Illustrate *of* APPL̄ ̄ORE

Including an account of one of its families

William Kingdon Slade and Annie Rosina

David Carter

Published by David Carter
1 Lansdown Road, Old Town,
Swindon, Wiltshire SN1 3NE

First Published 2000
Second edition revised November 2000

British Library Cataloguing in Publication Data
A catalogue record for this book is available from the British Library.

ISBN 0 9538524 0 7

Line Illustrations by Bill Wright, Appledore, Devon.
Designed & produced by Adrian Singer Design, Falmouth, Cornwall.
Printed & bound in the UK by Polestar AUP, Aberdeen.

CONTENTS

INTRODUCTION

I HAVE NEVER LIVED in Appledore, but of course this is my loss. I have however spent increasing amounts of time here over the years, and have come to appreciate more and more the atmosphere and sense of history which still exists in this small town beside the river Torridge in North Devon.

The quaint back streets, or 'drangs' as they are known locally, are a source of much pleasure in today's traffic-choked society, and the freedom to stroll around them is greatly appreciated, even if you do have to look out for the occasional motor vehicle squeezing its way between the buildings. Apart from that, and the odd gaggle of tourists who have left the main road purposely to visit the town, the only thing likely to interrupt your thoughts during your exploration is the slight embarrassment of peering in at people's windows as you walk past, and feeling that you are intruding in some way into their private world.

Although Appledore is not a seaside resort in the general sense, summer visitors who come here presumably seeking a quiet and relaxing holiday, create a bustle that is welcomed by those who make a living from them. Their own presence however does destroy the quiet and peaceful atmosphere that they have come to seek. Nevertheless, it is perhaps the sense of scale in the older buildings which is immediately apparent, and the community spirit lost in most other parts of the country, can still be seen to be thriving here. Indeed it is difficult to imagine a community spirit not being present in a situation where buildings overlap each other to the extent they do, and where you cannot quite shake hands across the street, but it almost seems as though you can.

The Quay, which has for a century and a half been the focal point of the town, is now busy with cars, and visitors eating their ice-creams, watching the children crabbing at high tide, and generally waiting for boats which have long since ceased to arrive. Indeed the recently widened quay seems to be a waterfront waiting for something to happen, and the pleasure is in wondering what that might be, or if it ever will happen. Looking out from the long stretch of quayside, it appears to have been built for the purpose of accommodating a far greater quantity of boats than actually use it today, as though optimistically expecting the fleets of fishing and trading boats which used it in decades past, and which are unlikely to use it again.

Sometimes the anticipation is rewarded, with a new vessel from the Appledore Shipbuilders yard making its first journey out to sea, and gathering a large crowd of onlookers in the process. Some will be there because they know that this is the life blood of the town and therefore an important occasion, others because they have been involved in building the vessel and are watching it go with sadness as you do with one of your children, and some will be there because there is a crowd gathering and are wondering what is happening. Other than that, and the yachts racing from Instow across the water, Appledore is largely untouched by the frenzy of activity experienced all too often in other seaside resorts, which is what makes the town so pleasant to visit.

The quiet and lazy drangs behind the quay, alas no longer cobbled, are fascinating in their timelessness, and it is not too difficult to imagine past generations of sailors walking home after long sea voyages carrying their possessions over their shoulders, and hoping for a rest period at home before embarking on the next journey. This is however a fairly romantic image of a past life which by all accounts was harder than we imagine it today, and I hope that this book will shed a little more light on the conditions which existed at various times in the past, but also be informative on the history of Appledore, and tell how it came to be what it is now.

So how can someone who has not lived in Appledore tell its history? Well, to say I'm an outsider is perhaps not entirely true. My father was born and bred in the village, as was his father, and four more generations of fathers before him. My great-grandfather made his living from ownership of trading ketches and schooners, and made sufficient money to build a whole row of houses in 1924, one for himself, and one for each of his five children. The house given to my grand-mother is today still in our ownership – the last one of the row to be maintained by the family. I have written this history to tell the story of the trade my great-grandfather was in, the village in which he lived, and how a hard fought existence in a small north Devon town came to be profitable for him and his family, and is still being passed on to subsequent generations.

The photographs shown in this book have come from many sources, and I hope that they will show how Appledore has changed, or in some cases, hasn't changed over the years. I have tried to be informative about each one, but a picture is the best way of illustrating the history of any community, so I therefore hope that most of them speak for themselves.

Above is the earliest known picture of Appledore Quay. Beara's shop is on the very left,
but the building next to it, still has the original lower façade, showing it before it was converted into a shop.
Gas lamps were brought to the Quay in 1875, and a collar factory was established in the next building along
in 1882, and may therefore have been in operation when this picture was taken.
The vessels lying off the Quay, are the *'Happy Return'* (left) and *'Countess Caithness'* (right).
(National Maritime Museum, Greenwich, London)

Below is probably the first ever aerial photograph of Appledore, clearly showing the peninsula upon which it
was built, and the two separate settlements of Appledore and Irsha. The date is about 1922, and some of the
many schooners and ketches that traded from Appledore at that time can be seen anchored off the Quay.
Many small fishing boats can also be seen moored in the distance. The church is easily identified, as are the
terraced houses in Alpha Place. *(North Devon Museum Trust)*

Docton House, probably the oldest surviving building in Appledore. Dating from the 14th century, it has served as a Cistercian rest-house; then after the dissolution of the monasteries it became home of the Docton family from Hartland, and was used later in life by Alfred Green for block-making, canoe building, and photographic studio work. *(National Maritime Museum, Greenwich, London)*

Looking towards East Appledore, the New Quay Dock, and the end of the Marine Parade houses in the distance. This is one of the earliest pictures of Appledore, dating from the 1880s. Note the belfry on the end of the building in the New Quay Dock, although this was demolished in 1950.
(North Devon Museum Trust)

View of the Bar in about 1890, which appears little different from today. However, the gravel barges on the sprat ridge in the centre of the river would not be able to land there today, as the ridge is now much lower. Note also the small mounds on the left of the picture. These are piles of limestone unloaded from ships, and waiting to be taken to the lime kiln just off the picture to the left, the remains of which still exist. The Coastguard House and Customs House are prominent at the bottom of the hill, and just visible is the roof of the lifeboat house. *(North Devon Museum Trust Collections)*

Appledore attracted Victorian artists, who seem to have appreciated the timeless quality of the village and the inhabitants. In the 1891 census, a landscape painter from West Bromwich is shown to be lodging in the village, and here in 1894 two more artists are on the beach below Irsha Street producing watercolour paintings. Note that only one of the children has shoes or stockings, and they seem to be taking a curious interest in the outsiders, except for the girl on the right, who should perhaps be concentrating more on keeping her knickers up!
The boat on davits behind the group is the chief pilot's boat, ready to be dropped over the wall should a ship need assistance in entering the estuary. *(Victoria & Albert Museum)*

This view below shows Appledore from Instow in the 1880s, and many ships are crowding the waterfront. The hillside behind the village has few trees, as a result of the wood-hungry lime-burning industry. Richmond House can be seen standing stark and prominent on the Hill, and the site of the Civil War fort on the highest point of Staddon Hill can also just be identified. *(North Devon Museum Trust)*

A 'lost view' of Appledore, as these charming cottages are no longer in existence, although their location can just be determined from the view of the churchyard wall and railings on the left of the picture. These buildings, known as 'Cann's Court' were demolished to allow the road to be extended to the north of the church. Joseph Cox is seen standing in the gateway to his cottage. *(North Devon Museum Trust)*

The same view as above, showing the entrance to Irsha Street, in about 1903. A road now passes through the site of these cottages, and the wall on the right disappeared when the promenade linking East and West Appledore was built just before the Second World War. *(National Maritime Museum, Greenwich, London)*

The old cobbled streets certainly added a unique atmosphere to Market Street as seen in these 'before and after' photographs from about a hundred years apart. This street was the centre of Appledore, acting as the main trading street, hence its name. Before the Quay was built, this street ran parallel to the water, with the narrow openings leading off to give access to jetties and slip-ways.

This is the lower end of the aptly named 'One End Street', shown here in the early 1900s, with a grocery shop window on the right. 'One End Street' was formerly known as 'Cocks Street' until about 1840, this name deriving from Cock's Field upon which the houses were originally built in the early 18th century.
In former years it was home to many mariners, but today the practicalities of living in one of Appledore's back streets are difficult, and many of the properties in streets such as this are now more suitable for short-term holiday lettings. *(North Devon Museum Trust)*

Irsha Street is a collection of properties surviving from the 17th, 18th and 19th centuries, and was formerly an ancient community in its own right called 'Irsha'. It runs parallel to the foreshore, with houses on the seaward side being subject to the force of storms and high seas against the walls at the end of their gardens. It was reputed to be a tough and lawless place in the past, strangers were attacked and there are reports of women fighting in the street. Today it is almost as quiet as it looks in this photograph from 1901, although this picture is probably deceptive. The street was the playground for children in Victorian times, such was the size of the families, that they spent most of their time outside in the street, or on the beach, rather than in the cramped and leaky houses. *(North Devon Museum Trust)*

The terrace of houses in Alpha Place seen here in about 1910 has changed little in the intervening years, mostly due to the surviving cobbled street. *(North Devon Museum Trust)*

Originally in Appledore, all main streets were cobbled, but today this is the only surviving example.

West Quay in Irsha Street in about 1920. The *'Royal George'* on the right of the picture is still there, but the *Prince of Wales'* closed in the 1970s. This Quay was the location for the West Appledore regattas in the 1930s, and has been subject to damage by the sea several times in the 20th century alone.
(North Devon Museum Trust)

Market Street in about 1910, but notice the 'sign' for the Globe Hotel on the left - a hanging glass globe. The proprietor of this hotel was George Moyse. On the right is the hardware and china shop of John Thomas Slader, plumber, and for fifty years the Parish Clerk, who served under four vicars of Appledore.
He also ran a chandler's shop on the Quay.
(North Devon Museum Trust)

Land's grocery shop at the bottom of Bude Street in about 1905. Further up the street on the left was a baker's shop. The same scene today looks very similar, except that the shop is now occupied by the Appledore Crafts Company, and the cobbled street has been resurfaced. The houses in this street appear to date from the 18th and early 19th centuries although traces of early 17th century structures can still be identified in amongst the later buildings. Bude Street was formerly known as Gaping (or Gapeing) Street, but its name changed in the 1830s. *(North Devon Museum Trust)*

An aerial photograph of Appledore and the Richmond Dock taken around 1960. Odun Road can be seen halfway up the hill, with William Yeo's Richmond House towards the top, and Look-Out cottage at the very top. The housing development on Staddon Hill has not yet begun to appear. *(North Devon Museum Trust)*

This traffic sign was specially made and positioned at the bottom end of Bude Street. It dates from 1903, when it would appear, traffic problems were not unknown even then.

The list of Buildings of Special Architectural Interest describes Bude Street as *'a very narrow cobbled street leading downhill from Odun Street to the Quay. Superficially it resembles the typical congested street of a small harbour town, but it is in no sense poor or squalid. It possesses pictorial qualities and makes a particular contribution to the atmosphere of the town'.*
This picture shows well-groomed young girls posing for a photographer in 1906.
(Courtesy: The Francis Frith Collection)

The same view today shows that the street has changed very little since then.

This picture taken around 1902, shows the formerly cobbled Marine Parade, at a time when there was no road access except from the end of the Quay. The bollards at the end of the street were probably safeguarding the doorways of the houses, which did not have any front gardens at this time.
The Custom's House shown here became the surgery of Dr Valentine, when the Custom's Headquarters was moved to West Appledore.
(North Devon Museum Trust)

Meeting Street in about 1905 showing the winding street leading up the hill, to Staddon and beyond. This was originally the main road into Appledore before Richmond Road was widened and joined up with the southern end of the Quay. In the 1891 census, this street was occupied by a ferryman, a pilot, two shipwrights, two sail-makers, a boat-builder, and about ten mariners. It also was the home to a smith, a bookseller, an accountant, a shoemaker, a builder, a mason, an innkeeper, a tailor, and a coachman.
(North Devon Museum Trust)

Meeting Street looking down from the top in about 1915, although the name of this street was originally 'Meeting House Street'. On the right is the Independent Chapel, built in 1816 on the site of the Meeting House which formerly occupied this location, and after which the street is named. The gentleman on the left looks as though he could be the minister of the chapel, and if the date is correct, then this would be Rev. Ralph Blake.

(North Devon Museum Trust)

The bottom of Myrtle Street in about 1900. The dock buildings surrounding Richmond Dock can be seen in the distance, as can the masts of a barque undergoing repairs in the dock.

The *'Dock Inn'* on the left, obviously refreshed many Richmond dock workers, but like so many of Appledore's pubs, it has now vanished, along with the *'Full Moon'*, the *'Mariner's Arms'*, the *'Prince of Wales'*, the *'Shipwright's Arms'*, the *'Tavern'*, the *'Ship'*, the *'Swan'*, the *Unicorn Inn'*, the *'Globe'*, the *'King's Head'*, and the *'Red Lion'*. *(North Devon Museum Trust)*

The photograph of the same view today shows just how much things have changed here, and you will note that this picture shows that again the road is in the process of being widened at the junction.

The corner of Myrtle Street and New Quay Street in about 1905. The *'Dock Inn'* in the centre of the picture is now demolished, although the locals often referred to this pub as the *'Drum and Monkey'*.
This nick-name apparently came about as a result of a sea captain who once stayed there, who didn't have enough money to pay his bill, so he left his Napoleonic drum and pet monkey as payment for his food and lodgings. The grocery and general provisions shop on the right has also gone, but the owner of this shop Kate Tuplin, is seen standing in her doorway; and the woman on the left of the picture is my great grandmother Rosina Annie Slade, probably going to the post box on the corner. The former name of this street was 'Old Post Office Hill', which was so named because a small Post Office was run here by Ann Hoyle from one of the houses until the 1850s.
The same view today shows not only the obvious widened road, but also the amount that the level of the street has been raised. *(National Maritime Museum, Greenwich, London)*

New Quay Street in about 1902, on the corner by the *'Bell Inn'*. Those who lived in the houses in East Appledore had large families in small houses, and some of the children have appeared for the photograph, although the boys and girls do not seem to mix very well! *(North Devon Museum Trust)*

Today, the scene looks rather different; the corner of the *'Bell Inn'* has been cut off to widen the road; the hanging bracket for the pub sign is still there today, even if the sign has vanished.

The cottages in 'Pitt' leading up the hill, are on an ancient track out of the village, shown here in about 1905. The same view today is easily recognisable, except that development to the left of the picture has intruded, and caused the road to become much wider.

New Street looks much tidier than it did a hundred years previously, and the standard of accommodation has improved greatly since that time. It still retains its atmosphere of old world charm though, and the traffic-free environment is a rarity these days, and sometimes most desirable, even though this brings obvious disadvantages. *(North Devon Museum Trust)*

Appledore Station under construction, but looking as though it is almost ready for the first train service from Bideford, which happened on 1st May 1908. On this day the station master Harold Moody received the train, upon which were many local notabilities making the first official journey on this line. The platform, new footbridge and other available spaces were, according to the Bideford Gazette, crowded with interested sightseers. *(North Devon Museum Trust Collections)*

The site of Appledore station today, and all that remains is part of the back wall of the station building, and Torridge Road, which follows faithfully the line of the former railway tracks out of the village.

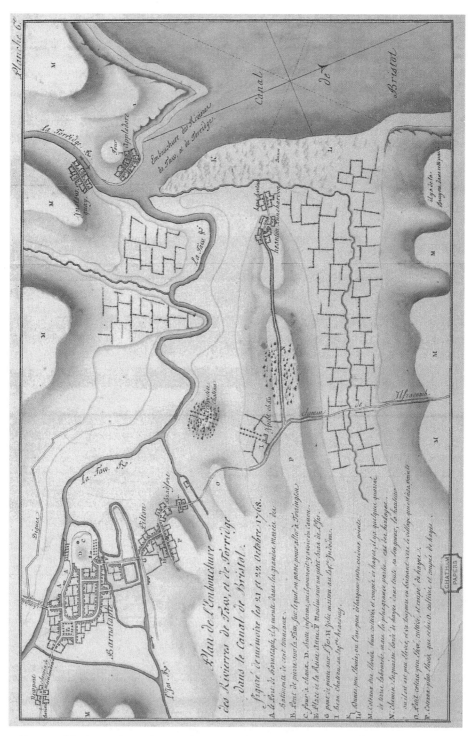

This map of the Taw and Torridge estuaries was made by French map-makers in 1768, and shows an
attractive but largely diagrammatic map of Appledore sitting at the confluence of the two rivers.
The map was probably made as a record of the defences that guarded our primary ports, and clearly shows
a tower on the hill behind Appledore. It is not clear what this tower was, although it could be the remains
of the Civil War fort guarding the estuary, or it may have been the large stone windmill which was
situated on the hill at Wooda a bit further inland. *(Public Record Office)*

This is the earliest known picture of the village, reproduced here from a watercolour painting by G Shepherd in 1819. It shows the division between the East and West halves of Appledore, between which can be seen the small chapel dedicated to St Anne, which pre-dates the existing parish church. The largest building at the top of Meeting Street is the newly completed Independent Chapel, and further to the left the waterfront of Appledore is shown before the Quay was built. The river channel also appears to be much closer to Instow than today. *(Ashmolean Museum, Oxford)*

CHAPTER ONE

History *of* APPLEDORE

APPLEDORE's location is a wonderful place for a settlement, with rolling Devon farmland behind, and two great rivers in front, and this has not gone unnoticed by settlers for many hundreds, if not thousands of years. Sitting at the confluence of the Taw and Torridge rivers, well stocked with fish, this must have been a fruitful place to live in the past; but for how long have people been living here? . . .

PRE-HISTORY

THERE IS LITTLE EVIDENCE of pre-historic settlement, although on the other side of the river at Fremington there exists a row of parallel standing stones leading into the water, assumed to date from the Bronze Age. These could well mark an ancient trackway, perhaps indicating the best place to cross the river, and show that people were living or passing through here thousands of years ago.

There is later evidence of a pre-Christian shrine, possibly dating back to Roman times. It is known that two small chapels were built on the estuary, one at Appledore, and one across the river at Crow Point immediately opposite. Both these Christian chapels were dedicated to St Anne, which is an unusual dedication, and probably derives from earlier pagan shrines on the sites, dedicated to Annis or Anu the Celtic mother of the pagan gods. Many holy wells

The seaweed-covered remains of a set of standing stones, at a remote location leading into the Taw River. The Devon Archaeological Society investigated these in 1932, and found fifteen surviving stones in two rows, extending thirty-four metres into the estuary. It was felt that they dated from the Bronze Age, possibly marking the site of an ancient trackway.

subsequently dedicated to St Anne were named after this Celtic goddess. Quite often Christian chapels took the name of the pagan saint to which the sites were previously dedicated, and in this way christianised them, and thereby we can see a faint link into the past, that is not recorded in any other way.

This chapel at Crow Point seems to have been on the route of an ancient salt works track leading up to Saunton, and again tracks such as this were known to be in existence many thousands of years ago.

855-860...

KING AETHELBALD of Wessex is recorded as giving some of his land at Braunton to the Abbot of Glastonbury so that the Abbot could have salmon for his house. Aethelbald is thought to have had his supply base in the Taw & Torridge estuary, because of the safe anchorage granted to any ships lying there, and because of its easy access into the Devon and Somerset hinterland, and no doubt other rulers of Wessex did the same.

878...

THIS WAS THE TIME of King Alfred's rule in Wessex, and in 878 he was being attacked on all sides by Viking invaders, and retreated to the Isle of Athelney in Somerset, engaged in daily guerrilla warfare with the Viking army.

A second Viking army was in south-west Wales with twenty-three ships and twelve hundred men, under the leadership of Ubba, and they sailed across to North Devon in a pincer movement to try and trap Alfred. By all accounts it was a fairly large battle, and it is said that eight hundred of Ubba's men were killed in the battle by the 'Local Viking Defence Volunteers' under the leadership of Odda,

In 878, Viking leader Ubba is believed to have landed near the Taw and Torridge rivers, with an army of twelve-hundred men and twenty-three ships, intent on attacking the rule of King Alfred in Wessex. Their incursion was met by local resistance, and a major battle occurred not far from their landing site.

ealdorman of Devon. No doubt many local men were killed, indeed a descendant of Odda recorded that the Danes won the battle, but were so depleted that they were unable to continue the campaign. This no doubt saved Alfred's bacon, and he was able to rally his troops in Somerset, and eventually defend Wessex successfully from the Vikings, and maintain the rule of the English.

The landing site of the Viking ships has never been positively identified, but if their boats had been swept up the Bristol Channel, the Taw & Torridge estuary might have seemed the best landing site. The raid extended a couple of miles inland up the Kenwith valley to an earthwork castle, which can still be seen today. However, if the Vikings had brought their boats into the estuary, they would have landed on the Instow side, and proceeded East, but the entrance to the bar probably deterred them, and the long sandy beach just outside proved safer as a landing site. It is therefore likely that Ubba bypassed Appledore on his

way up the valley, but after he was slain in the battle, legend has it that he was buried under a cairn of stones down by the river near a place which today is still called 'Hubbastone'. This cairn no longer exists, and is likely to have been either eroded by the river, or covered up by the Hubbastone yard. However the Devonshire Association Barrow Committee recorded the existence of a barrow in 1879, with a solid block of stone on it commemorating Hubba the Dane, and in 1889 a Directory still refers to this tomb as being 'nearby to Appledore'.

The name of the victorious Devon leader Odda is still recorded in the name of a road in Appledore – 'Odun Road', in which the Maritime Museum stands today.

1069...

IN THE AFTERMATH of 1066, when William of Normandy beat Harold Godwinson at Hastings, the political situation was far from settled. Harold's sons fled to Ireland still smarting at the defeat of their father, and no

After the battle, in which the Vikings suffered heavy losses, they took their slain leader to the riverbank and buried him under a large circular stone, on top of which they piled a cairn of smaller stones. This site is today still called Hubbastone after this Viking grave, although the stone itself seems to have been lost about a century ago.

Bill Wright 91

doubt threatening revenge. These three sons attacked Bristol the following year, but were beaten off after a lengthy skirmish by the inhabitants. Two years later in 1069, they sailed again from Ireland with sixty-four ships - obviously a well planned venture, and landed in the Taw & Torridge estuary. From there the army proceeded inland, but was taken by surprise by Eorl Brian who was ready with a similar sized army, which killed many of the invaders. The survivors fled back to their ships with Harold's sons, and were sent packing back to Ireland. This battle probably took place near Bloody Corner in Northam, as coins and bones from the time have been found there. This appears to have been the last attack made by the Anglo-Saxon followers of Harold, and thereafter England maintained the rule of the Norman King William.

Curiously, this is not the battle that Bloody Corner is named after; this being the previous battle there with Ubba the Danish chieftain, but which ironically probably took place at another location.

1086...

AT THE TIME of the Doomsday survey, the land as far as Clovelly is recorded as being in the hands of a Saxon lord called 'Bristric'. Appledore is not mentioned by name, but the manor of Northam has a fishery, and this can only refer to the riverside area of the parish of Northam, i.e.: the area now occupied by Appledore. The fishery up the river at Bideford was however worth ten times as much, and was then the most valuable recorded in Devon. The taking of salmon from the Taw and Torridge rivers can therefore be traced back almost a thousand years. There are also two saltworks in Northam, which earned four times as much as

In the Doomsday survey, Appledore came under the parish of Northam, but the fishing and salt making industries known to be taking place here must have been carried out by a small community living near the mouth of the estuary. The salt making must have taken place in Skern bay, which would have been ideal for this purpose.

the fishery, so this must have been a substantial industry, probably situated in Skern Bay.

1335···

THE FIRST mention of the name 'Appledore' in any document occurs in this year, granting a *'shop or stall next to the strand ate Apildore'*. Before (and indeed after) this, a lot of recorded history dealing with Appledore comes under the name of the parish in which it lies, i.e.: Northam; although when these records refer to shipbuilding or fishing, etc., they obviously refer to the area in which Appledore now lies.

DERIVATION OF PLACE NAME

There are various schools of thought as to the origin of the name 'Appledore', all of which sound plausible, and you can subscribe to which one you wish!

- Some say that 'Appledore' comes from a Saxon name meaning 'Apple tree', as in *'Apel-treows'* (apple trees) the treow being hardened into *drow* or *dre*, by the harsh speech of the Saxon tongue.

- Others say that the name is derived from the old Celtic meaning a pool of water. The Appledore 'Pool' is the safe harbourage for ships occurring at the junction of the Taw and Torridge rivers, which has been used as such for centuries, and lies just by Appledore, so this derivation is certainly possible. A very loose Welsh translation of 'pool of water' could be *'pwll dwr'*, and the Celtic forerunner of this may well have been transformed into 'Appledore'.

- I think that the most likely derivation is from 'Abertaw', the name meaning 'the mouth of the Taw'. 'Aber' means a river mouth, and Appledore is situated directly opposite the river Taw. The Devonshire Association in 1914 appeared to agree with this derivation, but you can make your own decision.

The earliest surviving written record showing the name Appledore (here shown as 'Apildore'). This document is a lease dated 1335 from the Chancery Archives, to say that John Rauf was granting permission to Geoffrey Fardel, of a shop next to the strand at Apildore, at a rent of 1d yearly during the first ten years, and half a mark yearly thereafter. John Rauf is to maintain the walls, and the tenant is to maintain the roof. Dated Sunday before Michaelmas, 8th year of the reign of Edward III. (Public Record Office)

1346···

THE CALAIS and Crecy campaign by Edward III in this year collected a fleet from all English ports, and seven ships and one hundred and twenty men were sent from 'Tawmouth'. This probably refers to all the ships from the Taw & Torridge rivers, but significantly calls it Tawmouth.

1347···

THE NAME 'APPLEDORE' occurs in a document from this year as *'Apeldur'*. In other documents it is *'Apuldore'* in 1397, and *'Applethurre'* in 1401.

It is thought that Appledore's earliest surviving building dates from around this period. **Docton House** is supposed to be a 14th century rest-house for travellers on the way to Hartland Abbey, a Cistercian monastery sixteen miles or so to the west. This stone built rest-house would have been opposite the sheltered river creek that has now been filled in by the Richmond dry-dock. There was probably a landing stage here for pilgrims arriving by sea – it not being possible to find safe landing any closer to Hartland. The relics of St Nectan were lodged at this Abbey, and

Bill Wright 99

Docton House is Appledore's earliest surviving building. Dating from the 14th century,
it is believed to have belonged to the Cistercian Abbey at Hartland, and to have been a place of
rest for pilgrims travelling there to view the bones of St Nectan.

there would probably have been pilgrims visiting it since its establishment in 1041.

1539...

THE 16th CENTURY arms of the Docton family can still be seen over the granite doorway at the top of Marine Parade. This crest is supposed to have been the work of Venetian sculptors who were over in this country working on one of our great mediaeval cathedrals. Docton Mill still stands near Hartland Abbey to this day, but the Docton family were not associated with these buildings until they were taken over by them after the dissolution of the monasteries in 1539. The upper room of Docton House was formerly known as the Banqueting Hall with plaster friezes and studded oak doors. Alas the building is no longer in its former glory, but it still stands as a reminder of Appledore's long forgotten past.

1540...

A TRAVELLER called John Leland passed through North Devon around this time, and mentioned Appledore as being a 'good village'. Quite what this means in our terms is uncertain, but he did note that there was shipbuilding taking place in the locality, with ships of up to two hundred and fifty tons being constructed further up the Torridge, and the existence of other trades that go with shipbuilding.

1565...

EXCHEQUER PORT BOOKS exist from 1565 for Barnstaple (which includes records for Appledore and Bideford), and these show that long-established trade routes were in existence. Records exist for merchants in Barnstaple (which are shown to generally use ships from Appledore) exporting cloth, and importing wine, dried fruits, oil and salt from Portugal and Spain, iron and wool from Biscay ports, wine, salt, vinegar, prunes, pitch and resin from France, sugar from Brazil, cochineal and pepper from Guinea, calico and spices from the East, and green woad (a dye) from the Azores.

Appledore had no surrounding villages producing cloth for export, so the village therefore specialised in building, owning and manning ships. Half of the vessels shown in the Port books, came from Appledore. The largest of these was a vessel called the *'Jesus'*, which sailed under a local master.

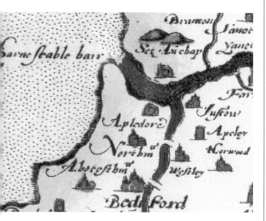

This is the earliest surviving map of Devon, and this detail from it shows Appledore in 1575, with a chapel indicated in the village.
Note that it shows the chapel on the other side of the estuary (St Ann's Chapel), although no remains of this site exist now.
(By permission of the British Library)

1575...

THE 'FATHER OF ENGLISH cartography' Christopher Saxton produced the first known map of Devon in this year, and it was therefore the first time that the village of Appledore had been shown on a map. It also shows 'St Ann Chapel' on the other side of the estuary, and further out is 'Barnestable barr'. It also shows that a chapel still existed at Appledore at this time.

1578...

A FISHING INDUSTRY was in evidence at the time, with many boats crossing the Atlantic to Newfoundland to catch cod. This is not directly referred to, as non-durable goods did not have to be recorded in the port books. However, in this year twenty-three tons of fish oil (which was processed from cod) was shipped out from Appledore to Bristol.

Salt was also an important commodity at the time, and the chief importer of this was a man called William Leigh (said to be of Northam, but likely to be from Appledore). He imported the salt from France and Spain, and sold it to other fishermen, so that they could send their cargoes of herrings etc on to places like London and Bristol.

1582...

THE POPULATION of the town increased during this period. We don't have population studies to prove this, but as the parish church records (at Northam) show that additional seating had been provided in this year, and again in 1595 and 1603 the people must have come from somewhere, and Appledore's thriving sea trade was the most likely source. This was the reign of Elizabeth I, when Britain's supremacy at sea was established, and provincial ports like Apple-dore served no small part in this. During this year, the number of ships registered at the local ports were:

> Instow - 1 vessel,
> Bideford - 4 vessels, and 39 mariners
> Northam (Appledore) - 15 vessels, and 115 mariners.

1588...

A TIME OF WAR with France and Spain, and the defeat of the Spanish Armada in British waters. Sir Richard Grenville of Bideford, took five ships from Appledore and joined Francis Drake at Plymouth. That Appledore sailors

Shipping was the major industry of the estuary in Elizabethan times, and ships from the Torridge joined Francis Drake at Plymouth to play their part in defending England from the Spanish Armada's invasion.

took part is certain, and tradition has it that in recognition of the bravery and courage of her seamen in the battle, Queen Elizabeth made Appledore a free port. Today it still has this designation, and there are no charges on ships berthing in the harbour.

1594...

FROM 1588 UNTIL 1594, there was an order prohibiting the departure of commercial ships from the port because of the Spanish war, which was still continuing. However in 1594 six ships were freed from the embargo, and sailed to Newfoundland to resume their fishing trade. After peace was announced in 1604, there was steady growth in this trade.

1596...

NO RECORDS of the slave trade have been found in Appledore from this time, although in Barnstaple a Neiger servant was baptised, as were two other black Africans over the next few years.

1600s...

IT IS DIFFICULT to give specific dates to many of the individual buildings in Appledore, although some of the houses in Bude Street and Irsha Street that we know today were probably built around this time. They look totally different from when they were originally constructed, as the frontages have been changed over the years, but behind the facades lie older structures dating from this period. The houses in West Appledore (today known as Irsha Street) were at this time a separate settlement, and not linked to the rest of the village, and it had the separate name of 'Irsha'.

1610...

THOMAS SALKELD, an English pirate took possession of Lundy in this year and pronounced himself King of the Island, shaving the heads of captured seamen and forcing his captives to labour on building of a quay and fortifications there. It was not until an Appledore man called George Escott, who had been an officer on board a merchant ship, led a revolt that Salkeld was overthrown and his captives released. Escott was granted a pension of eighteen pence a day as his reward.

1612...

IT IS RECORDED that twelve vessels brought cod oil back from Newfoundland this year, and eight years later, the fleet had increased to sixteen vessels. One of the vessels was built by a shipwright called Philip Cock, and sailed by his son John.

1616...

A TON OF LEAD from Bristol was discharged from a ship at Appledore, and stored at Docton House. This was subsequently shipped on to Hartland to repair the church roof. No doubt the Docton family were instrumental in this, as they occupied the nearby Hartland Abbey.

1625...

WAR WITH SPAIN broke out again, seriously affecting the fishing fleet, and again an embargo was put in place. However, for some ships the news came too late, as it was reported

that they had already sailed (they probably saw it coming!). This lasted for five years until they could again trade freely.

1630...

THE HISTORIAN WESTCOTE, writing at this time says that Appledore equalled other market towns for fair buildings, the number of inhabitants, and houses filled with good and skilful mariners. This town had increased within living memory from a settlement with 'but two poor houses'. (Obviously living memory got clouded in those days as well!).

1633...

SHIPWRIGHT PHILIP COCK died leaving assets worth £335. (The Cock family were still building ships in Appledore three-hundred years later, but were forced into liquidation in 1932).

1639...

A BARNSTAPLE MERCHANT had previously bought land on the other side of the Atlantic, and a town on this land became Barnstable (Massachusetts) around this time. It is also likely that other Appledore fishermen

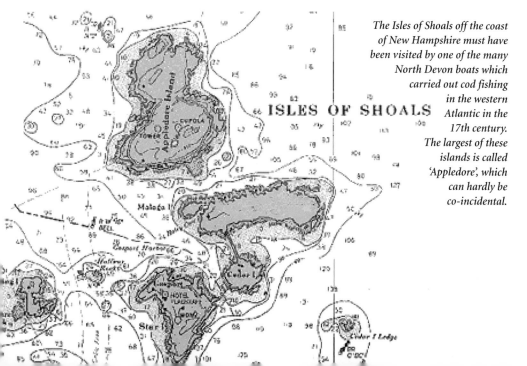

The Isles of Shoals off the coast of New Hampshire must have been visited by one of the many North Devon boats which carried out cod fishing in the western Atlantic in the 17th century. The largest of these islands is called 'Appledore', which can hardly be co-incidental.

searching for cod in the same vicinity found the Isles of Shoals off the coast of New Hampshire, and named the largest one 'Appledore', a name which still exists to this day.

1642...

AT THE START of the Civil War, many parts of Devon took the side of Cromwell and the Parliamentarians, because they had a dislike of the Ship taxes levied by the King over the previous ten years. Forts were built at Bideford on both sides of the river, and also on the highest part of Staddon hill above Appledore (near today's 'Look Out' cottage). In this way the Torridge river could be covered to best advantage.

The King's forces came up from Exeter, took Bideford in the July of 1643, and then proceeded to Appledore, where the initial attack was repulsed. A short siege took place before it finally surrendered.

1645...

NORTH DEVON remained in the control of the King's forces until 1645, when the Parliamentary forces began to get the upper hand again, and the Western headquarters were moved from Bristol to Barnstaple. Prince Charles (son and heir of the King, and later to become Charles II) was in control of these forces, and he visited Appledore on 10th July that year, when on his way down to Cornwall, and is presumed to have stayed at Docton House. Emergency mints were set up at various places in the country, and coins exist that are thought to have been minted at Appledore in 1645, possibly in Docton House, and the presence of Prince Charles seems to support this.

1646...

THE GARRISON on Staddon Hill had a large magazine store of weapons, and could easily

During the Civil War, Appledore had a fort on top of Staddon Hill, which was able to control shipping movements in and out of the estuary. This was of prime importance to whoever was in control, and was besieged and taken by the King's army in 1643, but subsequently attacked and retaken by Cromwell's forces in a bloody battle in 1646.

Bill Wright 99

control the shipping on the river from their commanding position. However, the Kings supremacy was failing, and Cromwell's forces eventually re-took Barnstaple and Exeter in 1646, followed by Appledore on 20th April. The stranglehold on the shipping trade was then lifted, and free passage of vessels could resume again.

1650...

THE FIRST EVIDENCE of non-conformity in religious services is noted in Appledore, with services being held in a barn near Bude Street. Twelve years later an Independent chapel was established by the Rev. Anthony Down, who refused to conform to traditional services in Northam, and came to Appledore to pursue his non-conformist views.

1653...

THE START OF PRESS-GANGING is noted in this year, when on 15th April the Navy Commissioners gave orders for the 'pressing' of seamen into the Navy. It is specifically noted that they would be doing this in North Devon at Appledore, Bideford and Combe, where it was known there were many seamen. Two years later it was reported that only twenty four men had been obtained as the others had fled upon seeing the press-gangs. In 1656, immunity was granted because of the Newfoundland fish trade, which was seen to be beneficial to the English economy.

1664...

THE *Rising Sun* Inn was built in Irsha Street.

1669...

A SHIP was wrecked on Bideford bar loaded with muskets and ammunition for Ireland. Charles II had an army there at the time, to enforce the Act of Settlement, so these were presumably destined for him.

1672...

IN JANUARY OF THIS YEAR, it was agreed that the Customs House for Bideford and Barnstaple should be sited at Appledore, even though Barnstaple was the home of most of the wealthy merchants, and Bideford had more shipping than Barnstaple. Appledore, situated in between both, was the place where most of the ships had to load and unload, and exceeded them both in numbers of shipping movements. However, as Appledore didn't have a Quay at this time, this Customs House wasn't authorised, and twelve days later, the argument was won by Bideford. It does show how busy Appledore was at the time, and how important it could have become.

The Newfoundland cod trade, although still large, was by this time overtaken by the tobacco trade, and as most of the tobacco merchants lived in Bideford, this probably explains this decision, especially as Bideford went on to become second only to London in importance in this trade.

1690...

SOME FORM of teaching children appears to have taken place at this time, as when Robert Kee died in Appledore in 1710, it was said that he had been teaching school for over twenty years in the village.

1700...

THE VOYAGES to Newfoundland for the fish trade continued. Approximately two hundred ships from Devon were regularly engaged in this trade, and no doubt Appledore contributed to a fair number of these. One of the ships was called the *Two Brothers* and was under the control of Thomas Chapple. With such a number of ships engaged in this, there would certainly have been a demand for seamen, and new men would have signed on at some of the Inns at the time, such as the *Beaver Inn* in Irsha Street, which still exists today.

The Appledore almshouses built by Thomas Melhuish in 1702, next to the Narrow Quay which existed at the side of the shallow sandy creek near Marine Parade. Similar to almshouses in Barnstaple, these were provided for the widows and poor of the parish. Although these were demolished in 1850 when the Richmond Dock was built, by this time there were further almshouses near the church, built by William Leigh.

1702...

FOUR ALMSHOUSES were built in East Appledore by Thomas Melhuish for the use of the widows of the parish. These lasted for one hundred and fifty years until they were demolished in 1850, when construction of the Richmond Dock commenced on this site.

1710...

IN THIS YEAR it was said that there were six-hundred families in the parish, and these were probably split evenly between Northam and Appledore, so an indication of the population of Appledore at this time can be estimated at around fifteen-hundred people.

1715...

A PRESBYTERIAN meeting house was opened in Appledore at the top of the hill behind the Quay, and subsequently gave the street its name: 'Meeting House Street', now: 'Meeting Street'.

1735...

MANY VESSELS WERE WRECKED on the treacherous Bideford bar at the entrance to the rivers over the years, so many that they are not often mentioned in contemporary accounts. One vessel wrecked this year was called the *'Joanna and Mary'* and she was sailing from Bristol to Guinea carrying wool-bales, linen and tallow. Her master and crew were drowned, but some of her cargo was able to be salvaged.

1740...

THE ORIGINAL CHAPEL of St Anne in Appledore (on the site of the present church) still appeared to be in use around this time, probably under the Roman Catholic faith. According to an old lady called Mrs Hammett in 1812, she remembered services taking place there when she was a child, and also remembered a burial taking place in the Chapel yard.

1742···

THE DEATHS IN THE PARISH during the summer of this year shoot up to five times the usual number, presumably due to a smallpox or plague outbreak.

1744···

A VESSEL called the *'Amoretta'* was wrecked on Bideford Bar. She was carrying tobacco from Virginia to Bideford for local merchant Thomas Benson, who lived at Knapp House midway between Appledore and Bideford.

1745···

A 'NEW QUAY' WAS BUILT at East Appledore near the home of Thomas Benson, who paid for it, and this construction assisted greatly in increasing the prosperity of the village, but mostly the prosperity of Thomas Benson! Up until then, the only Quay in Appledore was on the side of the river creek where the Richmond Dock now stands today. A new road was formed to reach Benson's Quay, and this was named 'New Quay Street' which still winds its way around the shore of East Appledore.

1747···

THOMAS BENSON (one of Appledore's most

Thomas Benson, local merchant of Knapp House, built this Quay in 1745 to assist the loading and unloading of his ships. He had inherited considerable wealth from his father including a fleet of ships plying regularly to the American colonies, and returning with tobacco, and this Quay increased his wealth and the prosperity of Appledore.

colourful and notorious characters) inherited fortunes from his father and brother, owned and ran about forty or fifty vessels that were engaged in the Newfoundland fish trade, and subsequently the tobacco trade. In 1747 he became a local MP, and was allowed to lease the then abandoned Lundy Island. He won a contract from the Government to transport convicts overseas, but instead of shipping them to Virginia as expected, he took them to Lundy and used them as forced labour walling, draining and cultivating the land. The contract was subsequently withdrawn!

1749···

BENSON ESTABLISHED a tobacco processing plant on Lundy. The tobacco was imported from Virginia on Benson's ships, landed at the New Quay, where he paid the import duty. He would then 'export' the tobacco to Lundy, and legally claim back the tax paid. The tobacco would be processed there, and then smuggled back to the mainland, thus earning him even more money. Because he had built his own Quay at Appledore, he was thereby able to evade the Customs control at Bideford. The Customs officers were at a loss to know how to deal with this, as Lundy did not come under the control of any mainland port, and they were therefore unable to stop him.

1752···

THOMAS BENSON'S downfall came when he hatched an even more dastardly plot. He owned an old Brigantine called the 'Nightingale', which he loaded with lace, silk, cutlery, pewter and woollen goods, and insured it heavily. It supposedly sailed for Maryland, but Benson had arranged for it to land at Lundy, where the cargo was unloaded under shadow of darkness, and the vessel then sailed off to the west of the island where she was set on fire and sunk. The crew escaped in the boats and were picked up. They were paid to keep quiet, but enemies of Benson plied some of the rescued crew with drink, and eventually the story came out.

1753···

THOMAS BENSON was fined over £7000 for smuggling offences, and his estate was seized as security.

1754···

THE Captain of the 'Nightingale' was captured and tried at the Old Bailey in London, and hanged there in June of that year. Thomas Benson escaped trial however by fleeing to Portugal, where he died in 1771.

1754···

A VERY GOOD QUALITY map of Devon was produced this year by Bowen. It shows the town of Appledore very clearly, in fact it almost appears to be larger than Bideford at this time, but that was probably a bit of artistic licence.

1768...

AN EXCELLENT detailed map of the Taw and Torridge estuary was produced this year by the French, who seem to have been making a study of our defences at all the strategic locations around our coast. It shows a tower on the hill above Appledore, and this could either be the remnant of the Civil War fort, or look-out tower that probably existed on the site of the current 'Look-out' cottage (see page 30).

1770...

MUCH OF THE LAND of Appledore was owned in the 18th century by a land-owning Squire called Roger Melhuish. Unfortunately he had money problems, and sold off parcels of land on which some of the houses in Bude Street, Market Street, Alpha Place and Meeting Street were built, on a two-hundred year lease set to start on the death of his son. Unfortunately he failed to ensure that this legacy was passed on, and when his son died without children in 1770, no-one knew who

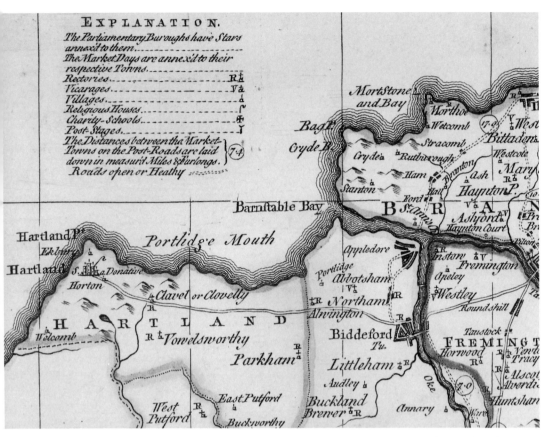

Bowen's map of Devon made in 1754, shows that Appledore was a relatively important place in the 18th century, with the street pattern clearly visible even on this County map. The road to Hartland used previously by pilgrims to the Abbey, is still the only road shown leading west. The River Taw is shown, but the Torridge has been called the 'Oke', (short for Okement) which is the other main tributary of this river, coming down from Dartmoor. By permission of the British Library, shelfmark c10d10.

the heirs of the Melhuish family were. Two hundred years later in 1970, panic was starting to set in when people wanted to sell their houses, and had to insure against a long-lost Melhuish cousin turning up to claim his inheritance. The situation is still the same today (applicants please form a queue!).

1770...

A SHIP called the '*Juba*' of Bristol was returning from Africa, and was wrecked on the nearby Saunton Sands. All the crew were drowned, but the cargo interestingly revealed casks of palm oil and some elephant's tusks.

1799...

SMUGGLING was not unknown in these times, and the Admiralty stationed vessels at Appledore to assist the Customs officers here at this time. The vessel sent here was a man-o-war called the '*Weazle*', and she was stationed in the area on and off for about twenty years until 1799 when disaster occurred. She was sent out to catch a smuggling party near Ilfracombe, but was caught in a north-westerly storm and driven onto the rocks near Croyde Bay. Her distress flares could be seen all around the bay, but no-one could get to her. There had been a party on board the previous evening, and presumably some people had failed to get home afterwards. The first body recovered was that of a young woman, but one hundred and five men were also drowned in this wreck which proved to be the worst ever shipping disaster in the North Devon area. Very little remained of the vessel, but one of her cannon still survives, and is currently to be seen outside the Maritime museum in Odun Road.

1805...

DURING the Napoleonic wars, there was a shortage of skilled mariners, and there were press-gangs operating (as in previous years) to find suitable mariners to serve in the Navy. Sometimes they were more selective in their choice. On one ship that was boarded off Lands End, Daniel Jenkins of Appledore was 'seconded' to serve because of his exceptional eyesight. His descendants claim that he was put on board the *Victory* and became one of her principle signalmen; indeed he is supposed to have hoisted the famous 'England expects...' message at the battle of Trafalgar. A Daniel Jenkins was certainly baptised in Northam in 1772, so if it were him, he would have been aged 33 at the time.

Another Appledore man on the *Victory* was supposed to be a man named Cox, whom Nelson gave the nickname of 'Warrior', and who became the coxswain of this ship. Cox later deserted, but when Nelson met him by chance some time later, he was given the choice of returning to serve under him, or hang at the yard arm! A fairly easy decision to make, and he continued to serve under Nelson until the famous battle.

(What great stories these are, and I am sure there is some truth in them; but on checking *HMS Victory's* 1805 crew list, neither of these names appear on it. No doubt these men could well have been at Trafalgar, but not on the *Victory*, and I have no doubt their descendants may have exaggerated their ancestors achievements over the years).

1808...

APART FROM Benson's New Quay, there was only one other Quay in Appledore at this time – called the 'Narrow Quay'. No one knows how long this Quay had been in existence, but it probably dated back to the 16th century. It was situated in front of the houses in what is now Marine Parade, and formed one side of a narrow creek that came inland at this point. It is likely that early Appledore grew up around this creek, which formed a sheltered haven for ship building and repair. Docton House faced onto this Narrow Quay, as it had for many centuries, but Myrtle Cottage nearby is also referred to in this year, when it was given to the minister of the Independent chapel for his use.

Further up the street, the road was later known as 'Post Office Hill' (now Myrtle Street), and there were a few cottages, but after that there was a narrow uninhabited lane leading up to the top of the hill.

1814...

APPLEDORE was transferred from the jurisdiction of the port of Barnstaple to Bideford. Until then, all vessels entering the Torridge, had to pass through the waters of the Port of Barnstaple. From now on there would be a shared entrance.

1816...

A UNITED REFORMED CHAPEL was built in Meeting Street in this year, to replace the Meeting House originally on this site. This building was described by Pevsner in his Buildings of England as 'relatively grand, with a rendered pedimented front, doric doorway, rusticated window surrounds and a bell cupola'.

1820...

MANY SHIPWRECK tragedies had occurred in Bideford Bay over the centuries, but it was in this year that Trinity House erected two beacon

This picture of the Northam Burrows lifeboat being launched in about 1880, shows just what a heavy task this was. Imagine trying to launch or retrieve this boat during a gale, with lives at stake, when the visibility and conditions were conspiring against you. Yet competition to be part of the lifeboat crew was severe, and to fight for a place on board, was not unknown. (North Devon Museum Trust Collections)

towers in the estuary; one on Crow Point on the Braunton Burrows, and one on the sand-hills near Instow. They are still there today, and still guide shipping in and out of the estuary. They came into operation on 10th November 1820.

1822...

THE Seaman's Bethel on the Quay opened in this year.

1825...

THE Royal National Lifeboat Institution was founded in 1824, and in February 1825 Appledore received its first lifeboat – certainly the first in the Bristol Channel, and most likely one of the first in the country. She was a 17-foot boat called the 'Volunteer', and was manned by four oarsmen. The first recorded rescue happened four years later, when a packet sloop called the 'Daniel' became stranded on the Bar, and the lifeboat made two trips out to her in treacherous seas, and rescued twelve lives. The 'Volunteer' lasted over thirty years, and in that time saved the lives of eighty-five people.

1828...

DESPITE the increase of religious chapels in the village over the previous few years, there still existed much superstition amongst the people. There exists a story about a man's spirit being conjured into a tree, which was then cut down and used to build Appledore Market, although quite what one is supposed to make of this is not too clear. The Market building was completed in the following year, and was known as a 'pannier' market, because the traders brought their goods in for sale in panniers, and these were arranged in a double row down the centre, and along the sides. The date '1828' and the letters 'AB' were shown on a plaque by the entrance ('AB' referred to the name of the builder: Alexander Beara, who owned the Market site).

1829...

IT WOULD APPEAR that Christmas festivities might have got a little out of hand this year. An anonymous writer to the paper says that the public carol singers became so drunk that they were incapable not only of attending the service, but of coming out of doors on Christmas Day, and that the money collected was only spent on feasting drinking and dancing. (No doubt one of the attendants of the many chapels in Appledore had a dislike for some of the others' ways of celebrating and felt compelled to write about it - how things have changed - or have they!?).

1830...

A DIRECTORY for this year says that the Gentry of the area had long been visiting Appledore to bathe in the waters and to inhale the fresh sea air. There were also a growing number of other visitors who came to Appledore for its quietness and ease. There were a number of lodging houses, and one good Inn, which was well served with fish from the local market. So, anyone despairing about the holiday-makers who visit the town today - remember that it's been happening for longer than you think.

No-one really knows what Appledore waterfront looked like before the Quay was built. However, we know that the houses in Market Street had their back gardens facing the water, ending in individual jetties and ladders down the sea wall, probably very similar to Irsha Street today. The gardens were extended and joined together in 1845 to form a common Quay.

1831...

A LIFEBOAT FUND was set up this year by Lord Rolle, to raise funds for the continuation of the lifeboat service, and to reward the crews for successful rescues. Over the years, various lifeboats were provided by this fund for Appledore.

1832...

THREE MEN from Appledore were caught and tried for burglary, which was common in the village, and were sentenced to be transported to Australia for seven years.

1834...

DESPITE having many chapels, the parish church serving Appledore was still two miles away at Northam, and there had been various representations for Appledore to be a parish in

its own right, and to build its own church. In 1834 the Bishop was asked to consider the case for rebuilding the old chapel which had stood on land between the two halves of the village. In this year, it appeared that the old chapel building had recently been patched up, but had not been used for religious purposes for many years, and seems to have been recently used as a cow-shed. This request took a few years to come to fruition, but eventually Appledore was to get its own church.

1835...

THE FIRST successful steam packet-boat service between Bideford and Bristol was established in this year, set up by local merchants and traders. The vessel was built in Appledore by William Clibbett junior, and was called the *'Torridge'*. She was the first steamer to be built in the area, and commenced her weekly service in February 1835.

1838...

THE NEW PARISH CHURCH of St Mary was completed in Appledore in 1838, but it was still under jurisdiction of the Northam clergy. However, six hundred parishioners had raised £1000 towards the cost of their new church, but they were unable to complete the tower, and had to wait another seventy years for this to be finished. Until then a small belfry with a single bell above the back of the nave had to suffice.

1839...

A STRIKE took place by seamen engaged in the limestone trade. Limestone was brought over

A common cargo on ships in the 19th century was limestone from South Wales. This was used in the lime-kilns to make lime for the fields and the building industry. Unloading the ships was an arduous task mostly carried out by women labourers. In the 1851 census, there were thirty-two limestone porters living in Irsha Street, twenty-six of them women.

in shiploads from South Wales, and was used in the lime-kilns next to the river. There were seven kilns between Appledore and Bideford, and women were employed as casual labourers to discharge the stone into the kilns. The strike created hardship in the locality, but worse was to come four years later, when the merchants reduced the wages of the female labourers, who eventually had to strike to insist on a living wage.

1840...

JEROME CLAPP became minister of the Independent Chapel for fifteen years. He set up a printing works at his house in Odun Road, turning out handbills and books for the Sunday School. Although he is relatively unknown, his son (born after his father left Appledore) became Jerome K Jerome, famous for 'Three men in a Boat', and other novels. He also had an interest in Hubba, and the alleged battle with Alfred the Great, and read widely on the subject. He read that under the 'Hubbastone' was a bottle containing a parchment giving an account of the battle. He went and found the Hubbastone on the beach (like a mill-stone, but six feet across), and with help lifted it, and amazingly found the bottle, but the parchment was decayed and unreadable. He is supposed to have replaced it with his own account of the battle, and put it back under the stone.

1841...

IN THIS YEAR a three-storey tower was built upstream from Appledore on a high point by the river. It was built by a merchant from Appledore called Thomas Chanter who owned shares in many vessels operating in the area. Many of his ships docked at Bideford to unload, and to save having stevedores waiting around for ships to arrive, he had this tower built so that he could have advance warning that his ships were coming over the Bar. In this way he had sufficient time to arrange for the

discharging of vessels knowing that they would arrive within the hour, and thereby save on the hire charges of the labourers. The tower became a prominent landmark, and acquired the name of 'Chanter's Folly', probably because after a time the trees grew up around it to block the view, and it became useless. There are other such viewing points known, one surviving one being a four-sided glass loft at the top of a house in Bude Street, built in 1817 to assist the local merchant who lived there get advance warning of the arrival of his ships.

1844...

APPLEDORE became a parish in its own right, and so no longer did the faithful have to travel to Northam to christen their children, get married and bury their dead. In this year also, a National School opened next to the church. Education had to be paid for, and I am sure the children appreciated it all the more for that! The cost was one shilling per week for each child, which when you consider some families could have five or six children of school age, was quite a lot of money. However within a year two-hundred children from the village were registered.

1845...

THE BIGGEST noticeable change occurred in Appledore in this year. Up until now, there was no Quay as we know it today; the back gardens of the houses in Market Street came down directly to the river, to their own sea walls, probably in the same way that the houses in Irsha Street still do. However, Thomas Chanter, the most respected merchant in Appledore at the time, persuaded the owners to club together and join all the gardens together and extend them outwards forming one Quay. It was a stone-faced quay, fully cobbled from end to end, and was a great improvement to the village. It was opened on 15th September 1845 with a public tea meeting, and became known as the 'Market Quay'.

The celebrations to mark the opening of the Quay commenced with the sounding of cannon, and the Bideford Town Band marching around the town. At 4:00pm, over seven hundred people sat down to tea in a large tent erected on the Quay. There were speeches, music, and the tent was decorated with variegated lamps, after which there was a display of fireworks. (North Devon Journal - September 1845)

Soon after this however, the owners of the Market Street houses realised that their back gardens had become valuable river-side property, and within a short space of time, new houses started to spring up facing the Quay, turning it into the familiar frontage that we see today.

1846...

SUPERSTITION still existed, and there is a report from this year of Richard Evans (14) accused of casting a spell over a girl who subsequently became ill for some time. The girl's father attempted to break the spell by dragging the boy to his house, making cuts on Richard's wrist, and performing a ritual to cancel the spell. The girl's father was subsequently taken to Court on assault charges.

1849...

SEAMEN'S employment was threatened this year when the government repealed the Navigation Laws which guaranteed jobs for Merchant seamen. All the ships in Appledore lowered their flags to half-mast, and an effigy of the Prime Minister was carried through the streets, before being burned on a bonfire of tar barrels in Chapel Field.

1850...

THE GRANDEST HOUSE in Appledore was constructed this year, on land towards the top of the hill, with views over the river and the bay

Bell Wright 99

beyond. The house was named 'Richmond House', after Richmond Bay in Prince Edward Island, where the merchant William Yeo had many business interests. The house is still there, converted into flats, but the grounds have now been built over, and the name of the house changed to 'The Holt', however the grandness can still be seen. William Yeo has been called the father of the modern shipbuilding industry in Appledore, and he wanted a large house for himself and his family. He had the road enlarged from his house down to the Quay, and lined the sides of the road with American evergreen oak trees specially imported from his lands in Prince Edward Island. These trees thrived, and eventually overshadowed the road so much that the locals nicknamed the road 'Dark Lane'.

1851...

THE Methodists, who had been gathering in a building near the Narrow Quay, built a new

Richmond House was built by one of Appledore's most successful merchants, William Yeo, and completed in 1856. The road from his house on Staddon Hill down to his dock was widened to allow him access, and today this is the main road into the town. In his grounds were many imported trees, and a fountain graced the front lawns.

chapel for themselves in 1851, facing onto William Yeo's newly widened road.

Also in this year, the Royal National Lifeboat Institution offered a prize of one-hundred guineas for the design of a new lifeboat, and they received two hundred and eighty entries from all over the world. One of the entries was submitted by a small Appledore boatbuilder named Henry Hinks, who came up with a design for a boat that would carry forty men, and cost £110 to build. It won second prize, and gained the recognition and respect of many who understood about boat designing. Hinks were building boats up to the mid 1980s.

1852...

APPLEDORE had three lifeboats at this time on various parts of the estuary. The third one stationed in this year was on the Northam Burrows, and was drawn by a team of horses straight into the sea beyond the Bar, thus saving time in reaching ships in trouble outside the river mouth. This service was used there until 1890, during which time many lives were saved.

1855...

CHARLES KINGSLEY, a local writer published his novel 'Westward Ho!', after which the subsequent nearby holiday town was named. Kingsley called Appledore the 'Little white fishing village'; however the local paper diminishes this romantic name, with stories of lawlessness; drunken brawls, petty thefts, attacks on strangers by children, etc. The first Policeman appointed three years previously was sacked in 1854 for fraud, and his absence this year does not seem to have helped the situation.

1856...

WILLIAM YEO, who had already built his house at the top of the hill, had been planning another project for six years, and it was completed this year. The open creek at the bottom of the hill, and the Narrow Quay, were to be enclosed with sea walls and lock gates to create a dry dock for the building and fitting out of ships. Previously all shipbuilding was carried out on the riverbanks under tidal conditions, but the construction of this dock meant that ships could be fitted out in half the time. The dock was called the 'Richmond Dock', again after Richmond Bay in Prince Edward Island where William and his father had extensive business interests mostly in building ships using local Canadian timber,

which they sailed back to Appledore for final fitting out.

This dock was most impressive for the time, being three hundred and thirty feet long, surrounded with a foundry, smiths' shops, sail lofts, block-making shop, mast houses, etc. It changed the whole appearance of this part of the village and several properties had to be demolished to make way for it, including the almshouses built one hundred and fifty years previously. The first ship to be launched from here was on 17th July 1856, and named the *'Elizabeth Yeo'* after William's wife.

1858...

IN 1858 another shipbuilding yard launched its first ship. James and Robert Cock, whose family appear to have been building ships in Appledore for over two-hundred and fifty years, moved into a new yard next to what is now the Seagate hotel. At this time, the Market Quay ended here, with a slip-way leading down to the river, but there was no road connection to West Appledore. Anyone wanting to get there had to walk down the slip-way, across the beach, and up the other side to Irsha Street. The Cock's first ship launched from this Churchfield Yard was a schooner called the *'Mary Boyns'*.

Also in this year a new Baptist Chapel was built in Meeting Street at a cost of £900, and opened on 7th July. Since 1835, the Baptists had been meeting in a hall in Irsha Street. This hall was subsequently bought by the Bible Christians, who used it until it was demolished in 1907.

1859...

A WEEK OF GALES caused thirteen vessels to be wrecked in Bideford Bay. A customs officer surveying the Northam Burrows afterwards saw a mile and a half of shambles of timbers, rigging, chains, cordage and sails, and it was said that 'there appeared to be no perfect article besides two anchors, a boat, two or three barrels, and a man's hat!'

*Over the years many vessels have been wrecked on the Bar at the mouth of the estuary.
In the 19th century one major vessel was wrecked in the bay on average every year. Lives were almost
certainly lost on most of these, and the wooden sailing ship has rightly been described as one of the most
dangerous methods of travelling ever devised.*

The Bideford and Appledore Dramatic Society was formed this year and gave performances in Richmond House, the proceeds going to the Church Infants school.

1863...

THE INTERIOR of St Mary's church was changed, adding stained-glass windows, with alterations to the chancel, flooring, railings, reading desk and pulpit.

1865...

LAWLESSNESS persisted in Appledore, but two Policemen were now appointed. However, the local paper included reports of women fighting in the street like starved tigresses,

tearing hair and scooping eyes. A couple of years later a periodical described the 'curious town of Appledore where inhabitants are as wild and uncivilised a set as any to be found in this part of the kingdom and where, till lately, a stranger could not pass without insult. Shoes and stockings are here unknown luxuries to the younger portion of the population and the women may be seen sitting outside their doors in the street working (or more frequently quarrelling) as is seen in the South of Europe'.

1870...

THE PREVIOUS reports did not seem to deter visitors though, and a guide for this year said that good inns and lodging houses were abundant to welcome strangers. There was a twice weekly steam packet service on the '*Princess Royal*' to Bristol.

However, gales this year caused fifty feet of the Quay wall to collapse, and urgent repairs were undertaken.

1872...

WILLIAM YEO died at the age of 59, and depression hit Appledore. The North American trade dried up, the docks were empty, and workers were left without jobs. Some tried to get jobs in other trades, and the smaller remaining ship builders kept the industry alive in the town, but Appledore was to face many years of gloom. William Yeo was buried at the top of Appledore churchyard in a tomb of polished marble.

1875...

A GAS WORKS was built to serve Appledore on a site beyond the lifeboat slip at Watertown.

The cost of constructing this was £3,500 and it powered sixty-five public lights in the town.

1878...

ROBERT COCK leased and then bought outright the Richmond Dock site, enabling him to expand his business into repairing ships as well as building them, and thus he succeeded William Yeo as the major shipbuilder in the town.

1882...

A MAJOR SOURCE of employment was started in Appledore this year. G Vincent and A Duncan, who had already opened a collar and cuff factory in Bideford, now took over a disused malt-house in a drang off the Quay in Appledore called Factory Ope, and also made fashion collars here. This factory was soon employing one hundred and fifty women, all the wives and daughters of the town's working men, and this increased the prosperity of these

Valuable employment was provided for the wives and daughters of the village in a collar factory which manufactured fashionable collars and cuffs in its premises on the Quay for forty-two years. Its heyday was in the late Victorian era, when many women were employed here or in a more mechanised factory in Bideford.

Bill Wright 99

families by having the luxury of a second working wage coming into the house. All the work was done by hand (unlike at Bideford), but no doubt the gas service into the town provided light for the factory, until electric power was installed. When fashions changed the factory gradually wound down, until it finally closed in 1925.

1891...

A HEALTH INSPECTION of some houses in the town showed that about forty were thought to be unfit for human habitation. They were shown to be without WCs, and many were still relying on wells for water, including some from their neighbours' properties. The inspectors were particularly appalled with the conditions of some houses in Irsha Street, and gave notice for these to be put into a proper sanitary condition.

1895...

AN ADMIRALTY battery and parade ground was built near the lifeboat station. This provided a part-time occupation for some of the mariners, and supplemented their income, which was especially useful if they were between voyages, and spending time at home repairing their ships. The opening of this gun battery was marked by a parade of a hundred local Royal Navy reservists.

1906...

THE DECLINE of the wooden sailing ship continued this year when Robert Cock & Sons phased out timber shipbuilding, and thereafter concentrated on steel ships.

1908...

A WRITER describing Appledore in this year called it 'a decayed port, a fishing village long past its prime. The Quays are reminiscent, and the whole place mumbles: "has been". The lanes, which are of the dirtiest, steepest and most rugged description, still retain their most ancient knobbly character. In short, Appledore is a curiosity'.

On a more positive note however, the railway came to Appledore in 1908, but it had been a long time coming. The Bideford,

For nine years Appledore had its own railway service linking it with Westward Ho! and Bideford. On its opening in 1908, much success was promised for it, but it was not to be, and closed during the Second World War. This picture shows the small shunting-style engine 'Kingsley' in Appledore Station in about 1910. (North Devon Museum Trust Collections)

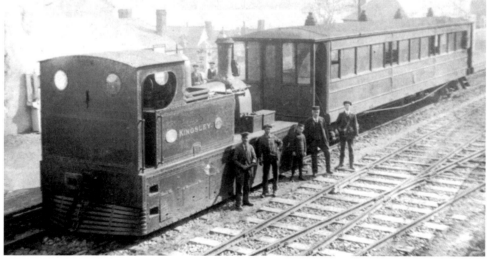

Westward Ho! and Appledore Railway that had started in 1896, reached Westward Ho! in 1901, and took another seven years to reach Appledore. It was seven miles long, and the trains were more like trams. Indeed there were three stops in Appledore itself – one near Watertown, one near the lifeboat slip, and lastly one at the station just to the north of the church. There was a celebration tea in the Public Rooms in Irsha Street, and great promises were made for the venture, but it was not to be. It was never a success, and lasted only nine years, the last train being on 28th March 1917. The trains were requisitioned during the First World War in 1917, and taken away. The line never re-opened, indeed the ship carrying the rolling stock to France was torpedoed and sunk, so that was the end of the Appledore Railway, although the remains of the Station building can still be seen in Torridge Road.

1914...

WHEN THE First World War broke out, the Royal Naval Reserve was immediately called up, and three hundred sailors left Appledore to report for duty. For those older ones who were left behind, carrying on their merchant shipping trade was far more risky, but more profitable now, as there were fewer boats with crews around to carry cargoes. The risk of enemy attack, and possibility of hitting a mine made it highly dangerous, but there was no safe option during these war years.

1915...

ON 4TH JULY this year, in the height of summer, there was a freak storm, when large hailstones fell on Appledore, and about forty panes of glass were broken in the Holt conservatories, as well as heavy rain flooding the lower part of the town.

1916...

THE LAST timber cargo ship to be built on the Torridge was the *P T Harris*, launched in 1912,

but unfortunately she was not to survive long. She was sent on a voyage by her owner Philip Harris, with his son Thomas as Master, and two of his grand-children as part of the crew. She sailed from Glasgow in June 1916, but she was never heard from again, and it is presumed that she hit a mine and sank without trace. All the crew were considered lost, and the only relic discovered was a life-buoy from the ship found washed up on the coast of North Wales.

1918...

THE WAR was over, but many seamen's lives had been lost. The granite obelisk war memorial outside Appledore church records the names of seventy-three men who lost their lives, forty-three of them being lost at sea.

1919...

A PICTURE-HOUSE opened in Appledore this year, when the Public Rooms built in 1894 in Irsha Street were converted into the Gaiety Cinema. This was the creation of Mr Hawkins, whose cinema generator also ran the electric lights on the Quay. This generator was housed underneath the cinema, and was occasionally swamped by spring tides.

LURE OF CONTRABAND

A TALE OF OLD APPLEDORE

BY
J. WEARE-GIFFARD

1920...

THE NOVEL 'Lure of Contraband' was published this year, and opens with the lines

'Dear, dirty, quaint old Appledore!' This was written by J Weare Giffard, and sub-titled 'A tale of Old Appledore'. It is the story of smugglers in the early 19th century, and is centred on the *Beaver Inn* in Irsha Street.

1926...

A DIRECTORY for this year shows that there was an hourly or half-hourly bus service from Appledore to Bideford from 8:40am up until 10:50pm. In later years, four companies operated these services: the National Omnibus Company, plus three local companies operated by Frank Hamlyn and Dave Hocking from East Appledore, and Sammy Guard from West Appledore.

1927...

THE BOOK 'Tarka the Otter' which was published this year by local writer Henry Williamson, now seems to set the theme to the whole of the North Devon countryside area.

Also this year, the most severe thunderstorm in living memory occurred over Appledore for about nine hours. One bolt of lightening, described as a flaming ball hurtling from the sky, hit Chanter's Folly splitting one side of it, and then went on to hit the schooner 'Haldon' moored in the river below, where it cut the main mast clean in two.

1930...

THE LONG-STANDING division between East and West Appledore became more tangible when for a couple of years Irsha Street held their own summer regatta at the small Quay next to the *Beaver Inn*. Later the whole village came back together for this annual festivity, which has continued ever since.

1932...

THE DEPRESSION YEARS had a drastic effect on the shipbuilding trade in Appledore. The wooden sailing ships were struggling to make a living, and no new ships were being constructed. Robert Cock & Sons went into

This general shop on the corner of Myrtle Street and New Quay Street was demolished soon after this picture was taken in 1933, to widen the road leading down towards the Quay; indeed the road widening seems to have already started in the distance.

liquidation in 1932, and the only other shipbuilder who continued up to the 2nd World War was P K Harris in the New Quay Yard, but they were only engaged in repairs and refits, and struggled to make a living for many years.

1933...

THE PASSAGEWAY between Myrtle Street and Marine Parade was widened by removing the large sail-loft building that was part of the Richmond Dock site. Later that year Tuplin's corner sweet shop was also demolished, and two-way traffic could now pass there.

1936...

IN THIS YEAR the *'Queen Mary'* regained the blue riband for the fastest Atlantic crossing from the French ship *'Normandie'*. Three of her officers and crew came from Appledore, and therefore played their small part in this historic event.

More importantly, this was the year in which Dave Hocking added the ice-cream business to his other business interests in the town, and without which, Appledore would not be the same!

1938...

THE ROAD leading down into Appledore was widened to allow vehicles easier access into the town. The American oak trees planted by William Yeo in the 1850s were cut down to make space, and no longer could the road be called 'Dark Lane'.

1939...

FOR SOME TIME NOW the old Market Quay had been crumbling away, and had been recently declared unsafe; the space offered along the frontage was also insufficient to accommodate motor vehicles. A plan was therefore made to extend and widen the Quay to form a more suitable frontage for Appledore. Work started on this in 1939, then stopped briefly when War broke out, but continued again in earnest when it was realised that this work was likely to be of strategic importance. It was completed in 1941 at a cost of £27,000.

Although the final result was extremely practical, it did not have the charm of the old curving wharf which matched the line of the buildings behind, but it created a proper road up and around St Mary's church, and to the rest of the village beyond.

1940...

APPLEDORE was made the headquarters of a resident Naval Officer, and this was given the name H.M.S. Appledore.

1942...

APPLEDORE became the base of training for Combined Operations Experiment Establishment, and continued as such until D-Day. Many experimental craft were tested in the estuary, and the knowledge of amphibious warfare was largely developed here, and this was to prove invaluable in the latter stages of the War. The capacity of Appledore's shipyards was entirely taken over constructing and repairing military craft.

1943...

THE AMERICAN FORCES arrived at short notice, and three assault divisions were being trained at various points around the estuary. By the beginning of the following year almost a million American servicemen were stationed in the West Country, and someone commented at the time that it seemed as though half of them were in Appledore and Bideford.

1944...

AT THE END OF MAY, virtually overnight, Appledore woke to find the river almost deserted. It was soon apparent what all the training had been for, when on 6th June 1944, news of the D-Day landing was heard.

1945...

ON 8th MAY 1945, V.E. day was announced, the church bells rang out, and bonfires were lit from the blackout materials no longer needed. Later, on V.J. night some excited naval ratings set fire to Chanter's Folly, and the interior was gutted.

1950...

IN THIS YEAR Appledore was used as the backdrop in a film. Walt Disney wanted to film 'Treasure Island', and so he bought a wooden sailing ship from South Devon, and brought it to Appledore to convert into the 'Hispaniola'. This was one of the surviving places in the country where the necessary skills were still available. Part of the film was shot in the estuary, and at one point the director asked for a dozen local men to be found and made up to look like pirates. An assistant was despatched and carried out this request, but soon returned and said 'they don't need make-up, they already look like pirates!'

1952...

'CHANTERS FOLLY' – the landmark tower built above Hubbastone Quarry had become so ruinous by this time, that it had to be demolished on 13th November this year, to prevent it falling apart and causing an accident.

1958...

APPLEDORE'S Gaiety cinema closed this year blaming 'competition from television'.

1960...

THE 2nd WORLD WAR finally killed off the

1950. The Plymouth schooner 'Rylands' which was converted at Appledore to the fictitious galleon 'Hispaniola' for the filming of Walt Disney's film of 'Treasure Island'. Appledore was just about the only place in the country where this work was able to be carried out, as the work was very specialised, and few other communities had retained these skills. (Copyright: North Devon Museum Trust)

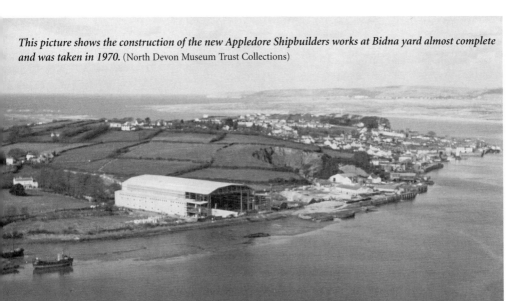

This picture shows the construction of the new Appledore Shipbuilders works at Bidna yard almost complete and was taken in 1970. (North Devon Museum Trust Collections)

shipping trade carried out by the hundreds of wooden ships in times past, but most goods now went by road, and sea cargoes were hard to find. The remaining ships were commandeered during the War for military purposes, and never returned to their former use. A few ships kept going, but in 1960 the last schooner, *'Kathleen and May'*, and the last ketch *'Irene'* left Appledore for the final time in their working lives.

1963...

A POTENTIAL DISASTER almost happened when the only main surviving shipbuilders in the town, P K Harris, were forced into liquidation overnight, and three hundred and fifty employees were out of work, at literally one minute's notice. A survival package was formed fairly quickly though, and a new company called 'Appledore Shipbuilders Ltd' was formed, and work again resumed in the Richmond Dock. However, if the firm was to survive it had to expand, and the Richmond Dock site was now too small for the kind of ships needed to be built and repaired. An extremely ambitious decision was taken to build a completely new

shipyard just up the river at Bidna. This yard would be covered, and large enough for the business to expand and thrive.

1968...

A CANADIAN COMPANY was looking for a shipbuilder to build a replica of an old wooden sailing ship called the 'Nonsuch' for the three hundred-year anniversary of the Hudson Bay Company. There were no skilled workmen surviving to do this, except for a few in Appledore, and Alan Hinks small yard agreed to take on the task. She was duly constructed and launched in 1968, and everyone concerned was delighted with the result. World-wide interest was generated by this, and according to the police, forty thousand people descended on Appledore to see this wonder for themselves.

1970...

THE LARGEST covered shipyard in Europe was opened, and on 17th April 1970 the first ship was launched from the new Appledore Shipbuilders works. She was a three thousand-ton sand-dredger, and never before had Appledore sent such a large ship out to sea from her yards. The following year the yard was visited by the Duke of Edinburgh who spent several hours meeting the people involved, and touring the premises.

1973···

FOLLOWING the success of the 'Nonsuch', Alan Hinks yard agreed to build a replica of the 'Golden Hinde' for an American Consortium. She was launched this year, and created just as much interest as had the 'Nonsuch' four years previously. She sailed to San Francisco, and then circumnavigated the world.

1977···

THE INTEREST in Appledore's maritime past was recognised this year, when its Maritime Museum opened in a large property in Odun Road. Without doubt, Appledore has had a unique importance in the maritime world out of all proportion to its size, and it is only fitting that it has a museum to bring due recognition to this achievement.

1990···

PARKING PROBLEMs in the town were helped by the completion of a large waterfront car park, built on reclaimed land in from of the church.

1996···

DUE TO dwindling congregations, the United Reformed Chapel at the top of Meeting Street closed its doors for the final time.

1997···

THE FLOODING of Appledore Quay on spring tides had been a problem for some years, even before the building of the Quay during the 2nd World War. In order to safeguard the houses in the lower part of the town, a flood defence scheme was designed, and completed in this year. The Quay frontage

was again reformed, with even more space in front of the Quay-front houses, and a raised promenade walkway has made a very pleasant addition to this much needed defence.

2000+···

THE FUTURE FOR APPLEDORE is perhaps looking brighter than it has for some time. The shipyard is still contributing to the economy of the area, the re-formed Quay and flood protection has given a new lease of life to that part of the town, and the interest in history and the places associated with it are attracting sufficient visitors to make tourism a major source of income for many residents. True, there are many holiday-let cottages in the village, but they also contribute to the influx of visitors who come and stay in this historic setting, and I hope that this book will inspire their interest in it even further.

Times change quickly though, and the future prosperity of a place can never be guaranteed. Attitudes change also: traditionally according to Bideford people, Appledore has always been the place where they eat missionaries. As recently as 1952, one local says that they would still eat missionaries, but they can't get them so easily now! Who knows what future attitudes Appledore people may have towards strangers?

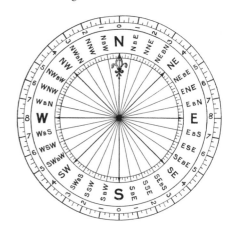

This picture was taken about 1895 and shows the grocers shop at the bottom of Bude Street. This shop and Post Office was run by William Land from Alwington and his wife Rosanna, and he is standing in the doorway of his shop. Note the hams hanging in the doorway. *(North Devon Museum Trust)*

The disused *'Dock Inn'* pub seen here in about 1920. It was demolished in about 1946 when the road was widened, and part of the front gardens of the properties just behind were also taken. Further up Myrtle Street, the wall on the left enclosed an orchard, on which terraced houses were built in 1923. The houses at the end of Pitt can be seen in the distance, and beyond that 'Dark Lane' winds its way up the hill. It was named Dark Lane because of the overhanging evergreen American oak trees planted by William Yeo to line the route from his house, down to Richmond Dock.

(North Devon Museum Trust)

The far end of Irsha Street shown here in 1913; the houses of Hillcliff Terrace are seen further along on the left. The presence of children is not unusual, although the fact that they are wearing shoes is not normal, and probably indicates that the photograph was taken on a Sunday, when best clothes, including shoes and socks had to be worn. *(National Maritime Museum, Greenwich, London)*

In 1908, Charles Harper wrote: *"Appledore's lanes, which are of the dirtiest, steepest and most rugged description, still retain their most ancient knobbly character. In short, Appledore is a curiosity, and one not in any immediate likelihood of being reformed out of that status, for it is at the very end of things"* (....poor Appledore !!). *(North Devon Museum Trust)*

The area just outside the Richmond Dock was known as the 'Parlour', and here we see several vessels moored in this traditional safe harbourage. The two nearest ones are the '*Margaret*' (left) and the '*Coleen*' (centre). Chanter's Folly is prominent on the hill in the distance.
(National Maritime Museum, Greenwich, London)

The tower is Chanter's Folly seen here in 1907, with all its windows, and was probably the last time the structure was watertight. Its location has been made all the more dramatic by being subsequently perched on the edge of the Hubbastone Quarry. *(Courtesy: The Francis Frith Collection)*

Chanter's Folly was a prominent landmark for over 100 years. Erected by local merchant and shipowner Thomas Chanter, it was used to signal to Bideford the approach of his incoming ships so that discharging preparations could be made.
Some years after he died the floors and stairs became rotten and rickety. A lightning strike in 1927 and a celebration fire on V.J. night by excited naval ratings finally made it unsafe and it was demolished in 1952, soon after this picture was taken. *(National Monuments Record Centre)*

These old cottages near West Quay in Irsha Street have now been demolished and replaced with more modern properties. A public health inspection in 1891 showed that many dwellings were lacking in basic facilities such as water supply and drainage, although when the inspectors suggested that about 40 properties were unfit for human habitation, this almost caused a riot in the close community of Irsha Street. The water supply was from wells, and these were often shared between properties. *(North Devon Museum Trust)*

This picture from 1912 shows clearly the width of the Quay at this point, and the flagpole erected on the edge, upon which a cone would be hoisted if a gale was imminent. Behind the flagpole (the cylindrical pill-box) is actually a newly installed men's urinal, which stayed on the Quay front until about 1930. On the right is the Seaman's Mission and Sailor's Rest. *(Courtesy: The Francis Frith Collection)*

Some of the many hard-working ships that traded out of Appledore in the 1800s are seen below at the turn of the 20th century moored up waiting for the tide. *(North Devon Museum Trust)*

The attractive Doric porch of Brabourne House, with the young lady standing outside still exists as one of the original features of the house in Marine Parade, this photo taken in about 1900.
(North Devon Museum Trust)

This picture below was taken in the early 1920s. The gardens of the Marine Parade houses were on the other side of the narrow roadway fronting their properties. Narrow passages linked Marine Parade to Myrtle Street at the upper end, and to the Quay at the other end. A narrow drang also went through to Market Street, but there was no other road access at this time. *(North Devon Museum Trust)*

Appledore Market shown here just before demolition in 1961. *(National Monuments Record Centre)*

Whilst the Market was being built in 1828, there appeared the following folklore story in the local newspaper:

"A very large tree was lately cut down near Hartland, into which it is reported by the peasantry of the neighbourhood that 'Major Docton' was conjured. The tree was purchased by a builder in Bideford, and cut into planks, one of which was washed away by the tide and drifted to Appledore, where it was picked up by some boatmen, and sold to the proprietor of the new Market then erecting. The real owner however, having heard where the plank was sent to, demanded it, but in vain. The bearer of the message strongly urged giving it up, declaring that as the Old Major had been conjured into it, it would certainly throw the new Market down. The words were prophetic for while they were yet disputing the subject, that part of the Market House containing the plank, fell with a sudden crash to the ground! The giving way of the wall is easily accounted for by less obtuse rules than those of magic; but it so astonished the owner that he was not as anxious to restore the conjured plank as he was just before to retain it".

(North Devon Journal: 29 May 1828)

Appledore Market was a pannier market, like the surviving ones at Bideford and Barnstaple. Originally the market had two rows of panniers on either side of a row of stalls, as can be seen today in the lower level of Bideford market. These were occupied by butchers and other traders. This view below of the working Appledore market was taken in 1930. *(Courtesy: The Francis Frith Collection)*

The original entrance into Appledore Market, seen here shortly before it was demolished in 1961.
The market buildings were erected in 1828 by Alexander Beara, who owned the site, and erected a plaque with his initials and the year, which can just be seen on the right of this picture.
The plaque survives in the back garden of the Maritime Museum in Odun Road (see below left).
(National Monuments Record Centre)

Appledore Market was held twice weekly on Wednesdays and Saturdays, and each was an eagerly awaited event in the life of the village. This picture inside the market has attracted the usual crowd of children posing for the camera.
(North Devon Museum Trust)

Marine Parade seen here in about 1905 seems very tranquil, but ships can clearly be seen in the Richmond Dock site on the other side of the wall, and the noise from there, must have prevailed in this enclosed street. Only a narrow passageway linked through to Myrtle Street at the end of this cul-de-sac, just enough for the postman, seen on the right of the picture, to do his rounds. *(North Devon Museum Trust)*

This old warehouse building blocked the route between Myrtle Street and Marine Parade, and was demolished shortly after this picture was taken in 1910. *(North Devon Museum Trust)*

These photographs show the wide open space of Marine Parade, newly widened and without cars, probably never having been seen so empty since these pictures were taken in about 1930. This terrace of houses in Marine Parade were all built in the early 19th century, and were extremely large and spacious for the period. The railings and the unified front gardens were only created however as part of the road-widening scheme.

(North Devon Museum Trust)

(North Devon Museum Trust)

This picture taken about 1890, shows a long demolished house with a passage underneath, and to walk through here was known as going 'under the bow'.

The upper floor housed a doctor's surgery, but this was all demolished in 1903. It stood in Marine Parade just in front of where the shop shown below is today. The house on the right is the first of the large houses in the Maine Parade Terrace.

(North Devon Museum Trust)

1940, Popham's bakery in Marine Parade. Mrs Popham is standing in the doorway of their shop. Such were the incidents of flooding, that this shop was built with steps leading up to it, in order to keep the water out during these extreme conditions. *(North Devon Museum Trust)*

This view of Bude Street in 1906 shows just how many children can be found for a photograph in this small street. It certainly seems to be an occasion, although the presence of a horse and carriage is probably less unusual than that of a professional photographer visiting the village. The man on the right may also have dressed up especially for the occasion in his militia uniform.
(Courtesy: The Francis Frith Collection)

An impression of the community spirit that prevailed in streets like New Street below, can be gained from a picture such as this one taken around 1900. Large families lived in these small houses, and the street outside was just as much a living area as the rooms inside, especially as the houses did not offer the degree of warmth and comfort that we expect today. *(North Devon Museum Trust)*

These two improbably well-groomed young girls make this an extremely attractive picture of Meeting Street, from 1910. The girl in the front is six year old Ada Scilly, and it is also interesting to see the other occupants of the houses making an appearance outside their doors for the photograph. The railings of the Baptist church are on the left, and the hanging sign of the *'Champion of Wales'* is at the bottom of the hill on the right.

Below is the southern end of Irsha Street near Ibex Court in 1905. Further along the street on the left, the Public Rooms were built in 1894, later to become the Gaiety cinema. Opposite this was the 17th century *'Rising Sun'* Inn. Just past the people standing on the left, lived John and Janie Carter who had 15 children between 1868 and 1893, and who raised them all in this house. The tallest girl in the centre of the picture is a cousin of theirs: Edith Carter.

(North Devon Museum Trust)

The houses at the bottom of Myrtle Street seen below before the street was widened in about 1946, although this photograph dates from about 1905. *(North Devon Museum Trust)*

The picture below from 1920 illustrates just how much the road widening of Myrtle Street was needed to meet the demands of modern traffic. The bus negotiating the narrow passage is Frank Hamlyn's 'Brown Bear' bus, giving a regular service to Bideford, and any pedestrians or cyclists in this gap obviously needed to take great care, such were the traffic problems in Appledore, even at this early date.
(North Devon Museum Trust Collections)

Market Street in the 1950s. Boyle's grocery shop is on the right, with the Globe Hotel beyond that (the glass globe has been replaced by a projecting sign). The bow windows on the left also occurred on the other frontages facing the Quay, but these have since been removed. The windows date from the late 18th century, and would originally have been shop windows. (*North Devon Museum Trust Collections*)

Market Street from outside *'The Royal'*. The cobbles have gone, replaced by a tarmac surface, and a central functional concrete drainage channel. The lady in the centre is Mrs Gayette (*North Devon Museum Trust*)

Odun Road has several large houses built in the late 18th or early 19th centuries. The road was named after the supposedly victorious Devon ealdorman Odda, who defeated Ubba and the Viking army in 878 AD. Today the road houses the North Devon Maritime Museum in the large house on the left, which was formerly the home of Jerome Clapp, congregational minister in the 1850s, and father of novelist Jerome K Jerome. *(North Devon Museum Trust)*

The southern end of the Quay in about 1910, taken from a boat approaching the slip-way. Ferries at this time were most important, not only to take passengers to Instow to catch the train, but to also take crews out to their ships anchored off the Quay. *(North Devon Museum Trust)*

Appledore Quay in about 1900. At this time, much of the smaller work done to trading vessels was carried out by the crews themselves, and here you can see a man shaping a new topmast for a ketch from a pine spar. At the end of the Quay is a high stone wall, probably put there as a windbreak. Note also the attractive bow-windowed shopfront on the right, which was the shoe and boot-makers shop of William Fursey. *(National Maritime Museum, Greenwich, London)*

In 1954, W G Hoskins in his book: 'A new survey of Devon' wrote that *"The Church of St Mary was built in 1838, and is dull; however, everything else about Appledore is fascinating".*
(North Devon Museum Trust Collections)

Bargemen and boatmen talking on the Quay in about 1906. The ketch in the background of this picture is the '*H F Bolt*'. The man sitting down on the right is Joseph Cox, and the man sitting down near him is Eddie Short. *(National Maritime Museum, Greenwich, London)*

Sometimes we forget that the Quay was a working Quay. Here men are straining to tie their ship securely, and many others are in the background working on their own vessels. The sounds of the ships creaking and the wind in the rigging, together with the smells of the cargoes, and repairs made using freshly sawn oak, combined with odours of tar and oakum, would have been very evocative, but are now forgotten here. *(National Maritime Museum, Greenwich, London)*

The final part of a journey home after a sea voyage, this ship's boy walking back to his house in West Appledore with his worldly goods on his back. His friends on the Quay next to the ketch 'Rosamund Jane' are probably pleased to see him back. The year is about 1915, and the two boys facing us on the right are Tom Schiller and Rees Scilly. *(National Maritime Museum, Greenwich, London)*

When Appledore had the old Quay, there were two slip-ways: one at the southern end where the ferry still comes in, and this one opposite the Seaman's Bethel. This slip-way was replaced with some steps when the Quay was reformed in 1940, but here you can see some boatmen hauling their boat up it in about 1903. The ketch *'Jane, Ann and Elizabeth'* is in the background. *(National Maritime Museum, Greenwich, London)*

It is difficult to imagine the numbers of ships trading out of Appledore in the past. In 1914 when this picture was taken, it was not unusual to see fifty or more ships sailing out of the estuary together after the Christmas holiday. In the Bristol Channel in the mid 1800s it was claimed that you could always see over three-hundred ships within sight of Lundy at any one time. Thomas Chanter therefore estimated that there were a million annual shipping passes of Lundy, which was possibly not an over-exaggeration.

(North Devon Museum Trust Collections)

Charles Harper, writing in 1908 not long after this turn of the century picture was taken said: *"Appledore is a decayed port; a fishing village long past its prime. As time whiles away its ship owners waxed rich in what the natives still call the Noofunlan trade but that was long ago, and it is scarce possible even the hoariest inhabitant recollects those times. The buildings, the quays are reminiscent; the whole place mumbles quite plainly in the imaginative ear "has been".*

This is by no means to hint that Appledore is poor or moribund. Vessels harbour a period in its docks, a quarry is in full blast on the hillside, and the fisherman fare out to sea in pursuit of the salmon and cod. But in general, Appledore has resignedly stood since the Noofunlan trade ceased, and remains very much what it was at the time of its ceasing, only something the worse for wear".

1930, and when seen from the water, the ships off the Quay look much bigger. The *'Emma Louise'* is on the left, the *'Mary Jones'* in the centre, and the *'Francis Beddoe'* on the right. She was owned by Philip Kelly Harris and was the last vessel to discharge a cargo at Boscastle in North Cornwall.

(North Devon Museum Trust)

(North Devon Museum Trust)

Appledore Quay-front from the other side of the river during low tide. The channel across the river is reduced to a few metres at times like these, and sometime it looks as though it is possible to walk across, but the currents should not be under-estimated, even on still days like this.
(North Devon Museum Trust Collections)

The Sailor's Rest and Seamen's Mission on Appledore Quay in about 1930. On the left was the Bethel (non-conformist seaman's chapel), and on the right was the house occupied by the minister. Through the door between the two (above which the words 'FEAR GOD' are just visible) was a downstairs community room. On the slip-way in front is the pilot gig *'Siren'. (North Devon Museum Trust Collections)*

Bargemen watching a Board of Trade inspector measuring an anchor chain on Appledore Quay. A boy is also watching, who because he has shoes and socks on, is probably a visitor; most Appledore boys went barefoot on weekdays. Behind them is the ketch '*Wolf*', so named because she was built to carry granite blocks for the Wolf Rock lighthouse, and when this was completed, she was bought by an Appledore man.

(*National Maritime Museum, Greenwich, London*)

This photo was taken by Mr Fox during one of his many visits to Appledore in the early years of the 19th century. Whatever was happening over the wall seems to be far more interesting than the photographer, who has captured this view of these men and boys in a wonderfully composed picture.

(*National Maritime Museum, Greenwich, London*)

A fairly busy looking Appledore Quay in 1903. Note the gas lamp at the top of the slip-way;
the gas works were built at Watertown in 1875, and supplied gas for sixty-five lights in the surrounding area.
The lamps were re-furbished (as seen here) in the early 1900s, and remained until almost 1930.
Note also the flagpole on the right, wrapped with barbed wire, to prevent high-spirited youngsters
climbing it for a dare. *(North Devon Museum Trust)*

This view of Appledore Pool, in the 1890s shows ketches lying in the mud waiting for the next tide, or the next cargo. The nearest ketch is the *'Nouvelle Marie'*, which is having some repair work done to her upper timbers.
On the right is a barque discharging cargo into sailing barges. Numerous small boys have also spotted the photographer, and have obligingly lined up to have their picture taken in the sandy puddles.
(The late Michael Bouquet)

Two aerial views of Appledore taken in about 1935 looking back along the Quay. Chanter's Folly can be seen on the hill in the distance, erected in 1841 to give advance warning to Bideford of ships arriving over the Bar. The Quay at this time stopped at the Seagate Hotel, next to which stood Robert Cock's shipbuilding yard. The long wide slip-way that he used can be seen leading down to the water's edge.
(North Devon Museum Trust)

The picture below clearly shows the layout of roads below the church, before the Quay was extended from beyond the Seagate Hotel. At this time a narrow road leads from the end of Market Street across to the beginning of Irsha Street. The large schooner just off the Quay is the '*Haldon*' owned by the Slade family. The ship behind her is the '*Lerina*', which traded regularly to Lundy Island. The engineer of the '*Lerina*' was Tom Hornabrook who later became chief mechanic of the Appledore lifeboat. *(North Devon Museum Trust)*

In the book 'Payne's Devon', describing Devon through the watercolours of William Payne, it says that: *"Early Victorian architecture is common in the old parts, six-panel doors and sash windows were in vogue for both old and new houses. Today Appledore is a fascinating labyrinth of narrow passages and courts, with delightful views across the estuary to Instow and Braunton sands".* This turn of the century photo of the Quay has a timeless quality that illustrates this romantic description particularly well. *(North Devon Museum Trust Collections)*

This photo shows what a block-makers shop looked like in the 1870s. Pulley blocks were complicated and a typical ketch or schooner needed several dozen of these, so making them was a specialised trade. This block-making and spar shop was owned by Philip Green, and situated in Docton House in Marine Parade. *(North Devon Museum Trust Collections)*

Alexander Beara's workshop on the Quay where they made 'Williams Patent reefing gear'.
This photograph from about 1920 shows Alexander Beara at the back, just right of centre. The man in the right foreground is William Smallridge, and the boy on the left George Batho. *(North Devon Museum Trust)*

Below is one of the small boat building and repair shops of which there were many in Appledore.
This photograph was taken in 1897, and shows James Channon and his son Richard working in their workshop on Appledore Quay (near to today's Post Office). *(North Devon Museum Trust)*

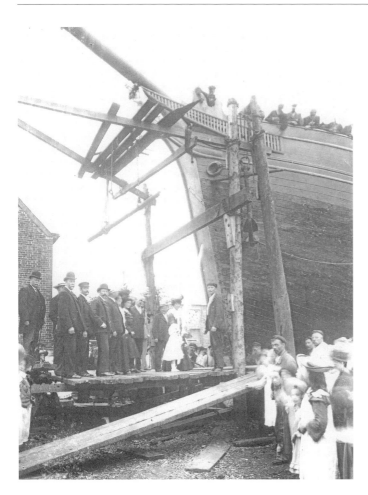

These two photographs show the launching in 1905 of the three-masted schooner *'Rose'* from the Bell Inn slip. She was built in the shipyard of Robert Cock & Sons, and the launching of any ship was always an occasion to be celebrated, as can be seen here.
(North Devon Museum Trust Collections)

(North Devon Museum Trust Collections)

The brigantine *'Clio'* built by Robert Cock and Sons in the New Quay yard. This is the launching ceremony for her in 1894. *(National Maritime Museum, Greenwich, London)*

These shipworkers below are working on the ketch *'Acacia'*, which has been laid up for routine work in 1906. Thomas Lock (my great great grandfather) who is on the left is spinning oakum for caulking the joints of the timbers, and Capt. Stanley Rogers and his mate George Dendle from Braunton are sealing the joints with pitch. *(National Maritime Museum, Greenwich, London)*

This photo taken in about 1885 shows two barques in Richmond Dock for repair. One of the barques is timber, the other steel. The bowsprit of the outer boat hangs over the end wall of the dock, in order to fit them both in. The foreman of the yard, Mr Hookway is standing on the left of the picture.

Outside the Richmond Dock was the Parlour, shown below in 1903. The dock was constructed between 1850 and 1856 by William Yeo to service and fit-out ships that had been built in his yards in Prince Edward Island. The site was originally a creek with a quay running along the north side of it, but the site William Yeo wanted was owned by various people, and it took some time to persuade the owners to sell their part of the land.
(North Devon Museum Trust)

This picture from 1890 shows the home and yard of George Edward Parkin, a yacht and small boat builder who moved from Barnstaple to Appledore in the 1850s, and set up his premises in Ibex Court, off Irsha Street. There were many such small boat building shops such as this in Appledore in the 19th century.

(National Maritime Museum, Greenwich, London)

The tea celebration below is taking place aboard an unknown sailing vessel in Richmond Dock in about 1900, presumably to mark the completion of her fitting out. *(National Maritime Museum, Greenwich, London)*

This is Pen Oatway's sail-loft in the 1930s. He is shown making a mizzen sail for Charles Lamey, skipper of the ketch '*Hobah*'. Sailmaking was a specialist trade, and often the larger sailing vessels of previous centuries had a sailmaker on board who was an ordinary seaman, but was also able to make any repairs that were needed on a long voyage. *(North Devon Museum Trust Collections)*

William Alexander Braund, sailmaker (left), learned his trade in a seven year apprenticeship in an Appledore sail loft, and serving at sea on square-rigged sailing ships. He lived in Appledore until the early 1900s when he moved to Braunton and set up his own sailmaking business. He is seen below in his 70s, with his family, working on the mainsail for a ketch. *(R L Knight Photographers)*

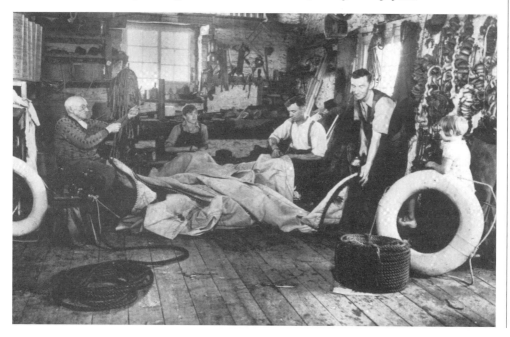

Appledore sailors being taken out to their ship by a local boatman, probably going to more than one ship if the numbers of sailors is anything to go by. One of the traditional methods of 'rowing' a boat is shown here, ie: sculling over the stern. The year is 1903. *(National Maritime Museum, Greenwich, London)*

(National Maritime Museum, Greenwich, London)

Here we see Gribble's Point and Tavern Corner – names mostly unknown now to Appledore people. Gribble's Point was the jutting out spur of land at this end of the Quay. This was the abrupt end to Appledore Quay at the Grand Hotel (now the Seagate Hotel) up until 1940, and the end wall can be seen in this picture. To the right of this used to be Robert Cock's shipbuilding business at Churchfield yard; and in the foreground is a working lug-sail boat. Next to the Grand Hotel is seen the haircutting and shaving saloon of Reuben Smith, whose signs on his wall announced his trade in English and French (Coupe de Cheveux). *(National Maritime Museum, Greenwich, London)*

Children playing at the bottom of the Quay slip-way in about 1902, and not only boys, but girls also. The scene on the water behind them looks busy, and these children will grow up quite at home amongst the bustle of life on the water.
(National Maritime Museum, Greenwich, London)

Salmon fishermen in the estuary in about 1905, this picture taken by Mr Fox. The traditional way of netting salmon in the Torridge river has probably not changed much in centuries, and the sight of fishermen mending their nets at the water's edge or on the Quay, would be a sight that mediaeval fishermen would be quite at home with. *(National Maritime Museum, Greenwich, London)*

Here we see two ladies about to catch the ferry, presumably to Instow. The ferryman is well known: he is William (Daddy) Johns, seen here still running the ferry whilst well into his seventies. The ladies are visitors however, and have been identified as Emma Bonnet from Worcestershire, and her niece Lucy Osbeck from South Wales. They were fairly regular visitors to Appledore in the 1900s, and were known to be finding out about ancestors of theirs who had lived in Meeting Street in the 1840s.
(National Maritime Museum, Greenwich, London)

A large number of people are seen walking along the Quay in this picture from about 1902. Quite what they are all doing is not clear, but many are dressed smartly, so it is probably a Sunday or other special occasion. *(National Maritime Museum, Greenwich, London)*

On Instow sands looking towards Appledore in the 1900s. Picture taken by Mr Fox. The trees on the hill behind the village have grown considerably since the picture taken about twenty years previously (shown on page 10). *(National Maritime Museum, Greenwich, London)*

The same two visiting ladies seen previously on page 100, are walking towards the ferry to take them to Instow, for a pleasure trip. The year is 1904. Also note the gravel barges anchored in the river.
(National Maritime Museum, Greenwich, London)

A boy visitor to Appledore taking his little sister down the slip-way in about 1902. The men near them are Isaac Craner (right) and William Short (left), both bargemen. The vessel against the Quay is the trading smack *'Rosamund Jane'*, the last vessel to trade into Hartland Quay before the Quay was destroyed by gales in the 1890s. *(National Maritime Museum, Greenwich, London)*

The Quay in about 1923 with various vessels lying at anchor. The two nearest ones are the *'Francis Beddoe'* (left) and the *'Humility'* (right). The centre of the three men is Thomas Powe, who owned the ketch *'Humility'*. However, she is seen here at the end of her working life, and never went to sea again after this picture was taken. *(National Maritime Museum, Greenwich, London)*

In the early 20th century when this picture below was taken, the Quay ended at the Seagate Hotel. Many generations of sailors must have been waved off from this point, where they could be seen sailing over the Bar, and into the Bideford Bay beyond. *(National Maritime Museum, Greenwich, London)*

The Quay slip-way in about 1905, picture taken by Mr Fox. The barrels at the top of the slip were owned by J Beara - chandler, and contained oil (for the ship's lamps). The young man in the centre with the white collar is Fred Hobbs, and the ferryman with the felt hat at the bottom of the slip is William Bailey.
(National Maritime Museum, Greenwich, London)

Boys will be boys, and in Appledore, boys were always on or near the water, as this W Fox picture from 1904 testifies. The three boys on the right are Tom Berry (12), George Lamey (10), and Bill Jillings (9), but the others are unknown. How curious to our eyes that children at that time never seemed to have shoes and socks, but always appeared to have caps! *(National Maritime Museum, Greenwich, London)*

Appledore Quay in 1932, and about nine ketches are seen moored near the Quay. There seems to be plenty of activity with men and women going out to them in boats, and it certainly looks as though some of them will be leaving on the tide. *(Courtesy: The Francis Frith Collection)*

Beara's hardware and chandlery business was started in 1830 by Alexander Beara in this shop on the Quay (now a supermarket), and survived for over a hundred years. John Beara is seen standing in the doorway of his shop in this picture from about 1910. The Beara family originally owned the land at this end of the Quay, including that section of the Quay itself, and the prominent rock that exists at low tide on the foreshore.
(North Devon Museum Trust)

Although not the collar factory on Appledore Quay, these pictures of the same company's factory in Bideford show the type of employment on offer to women in the early part of the 20th century. Many Appledore women worked in the Bideford factory, walking the two and a half miles there and back every day. The machine and pressing rooms here are greatly mechanised, but the factory in Appledore relied on all the work being done by hand, and so could not match the production of the Bideford factory.

(Kind permission: Shirley Hocking)

(Kind permission: Shirley Hocking)

A postcard from the early 1930s showing picturesque scenes of Appledore.
(North Devon Museum Trust Collections)

Many of the pictures from the early 20th century were taken by a regular visitor from Cardiff. Mr Fox, and his wife and son, spent their summers in Appledore from about 1900 to 1910, and being a keen photographer, he produced many familiar images of the village. This one shows his son (W C Fox) on board the ferry with 'Daddy' Johns. In later years W C Fox presented his father's photographs to the National Maritime Museum in London.
(National Maritime Museum, Greenwich, London)

Gravel barges such as these were commonplace in the river as working boats in the 19th and early 20th centuries. Gravel was taken from the ridges in the estuary and loaded into these boats at low tide. The barges here are loading at low water, and then waiting for the tide to come in, so that they can bring their cargo to the Quay to discharge. The ridges in the estuary have now been almost completely taken away because of this trade. *(North Devon Museum Trust Collections)*

(National Maritime Museum, Greenwich, London)

A gravel barge at the Quay here in 1890. Her name was the *'William'* but was more commonly known as the *'Irish Whiskey'*, Archibald Brend, bargeman, is seen on board. *(North Devon Museum Trust Collections)*

Seven Appledore boys caught here by photographer Mr Fox in 1904 sitting on a fence, most of them, as usual, barefoot. They are (left to right) Percy Powe, Morish Powe, S. Peake, William Blackmore, John Hammett, Edwin Yeo, and John Henry Peake.

(National Maritime Museum, Greenwich, London)

A poor quality photograph, but it serves to show the effect that the sea can have on apparently solid quay walls. This was the main Appledore Quay after a storm in February 1925, when a section on the slip-way collapsed due to battering by the water, and undermining of the support from behind. The 'Hanson Memorial Sailor's Rest' is in the background. *(North Devon Museum Trust Collections)*

Storm damage to the Quay wall at West Appledore, this picture also taken in 1925, from the *'Beaver Inn'*, and looking at the frantic activity to repair as much as possible before the next tide. Note the *'Prince of Wales'* pub in the background, and the damaged garden wall of the house immediately behind the wall breach. *(North Devon Museum Trust)*

The same storm damage in 1925 shown here from the other side. Note the *'Beaver Inn'* in the background, and how this has changed. *(North Devon Museum Trust Collections)*

Further damage to the sea wall at West Quay, this time in 1974. The road closure which resulted, caused more disruption than in previous occurrences of this nature, due to the greater reliance on motor transport to this street. The clean-up and repairs seen here will cause the road to be unusable for some time. *(North Devon Museum Trust Collections)*

This curious house was the home of Richard Blackmore and was situated next to the riverbank at Hubbastone. It was built from the deck-houses of 'HMS Delaware', which was broken up at Appledore in 1881, and the house was therefore called 'Delaware Cottage'. The picture above was taken soon after its construction, Richard Blackmore is on the right of the picture, and his wife Susan Blackmore (nee Carter) is sitting down at the back.
(North Devon Museum Trust Collections)

The later picture on the left shows that a veranda and pitched roofs has been added. Chanter's Folly can be seen above the quarry behind the house, and in the foreground many timbers are seasoning, that will be used for ship-building and repair. The house was demolished when the Hubbastone Yard was built.

(National Maritime Museum, Greenwich, London)

In 1845 Thomas Chanter's plan of joining the back gardens of the houses in Market Street together to form a unified Quay came to fruition, and there was a grand opening on the 15th September, with an open-air tea. This admission ticket survived thanks to the Beara family who owned the Market and other land at the south end of the Quay.

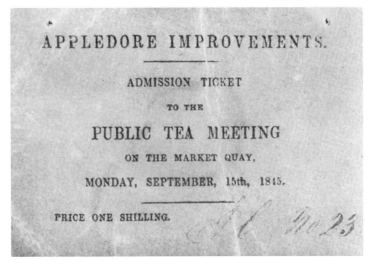

APPLEDORE IMPROVEMENTS.

ADMISSION TICKET

TO THE

PUBLIC TEA MEETING

ON THE MARKET QUAY,

MONDAY, SEPTEMBER, 15th, 1845.

PRICE ONE SHILLING.

The tea must have been a grand celebration, but remember that there would have been only a few houses fronting the Quay at this time, as they were mostly constructed afterwards. By the time of the 1851 census however, there were 15 inhabited properties fronting what was then called 'Victoria Quay'. *(North Devon Museum Trust Collections)*

This picture on the left clearly shows the line of the curved original Quay front, which matched the line of the buildings. This picture was taken from the upper window of Beara's shop in the late 1920s. Note the line of timber mooring posts set in from the edge of the Quay. *(North Devon Museum Trust)*

These ladies in 1904 are gathering seaweed from the shore, for food, which seems a rather curious occupation. However, there is a variety of seaweed that is edible, and which after washing and boiling is known as 'laver', and is something of a local delicacy. A directory of 1889 says that *"In Appledore the species of seaweed called laver is much in request"*. This was no doubt one of the items that you could purchase from the Market twice weekly. The ladies are: Mary Jewell, Hester Screech and Mary Tune.
(North Devon Museum Trust)

Scraping a living by harvesting the sea-shore. Here two men are gathering seaweed from the beach and loading in onto a cart, but in quantities too great to be of the edible variety.
This seaweed will be destined for the fields to act as a fertiliser. Picture taken in about 1905.
(National Maritime Museum, Greenwich, London)

Appledore, being at the mouth of the Taw and Torridge, was always in the forefront of saving lives in the event of any ships being in trouble in the estuary. Many ships got into trouble on the Bar, or in the sea outside the Bar, but the lifeboat stationed at Appledore often took too long to reach them. Lifeboats were therefore also stationed at each side of the estuary mouth, and launched directly into the sea by teams of horses as seen in these pictures showing the Northam Burrows boat being launched. This lifeboat station was established in 1852, but was closed in 1897, after eight separate boats had been stationed here. The horses used for launching the boats were kept at the farm opposite Hinks boatyard, and would jump the fence when they heard the maroons, and gallop by themselves to the boathouse.

(North Devon Museum Trust Collections)

Below is the Braunton Burrows lifeboat shed, with the lifeboat ready to be launched.

(North Devon Museum Trust Collections)

The slip-way at Badstep in about 1910. The lifeboat house is on the right with the Custom's House behind. Local historian Charles Chappell and his wife gave the land upon which the lifeboat house stands to the RNLI in 1889. *(North Devon Museum Trust)*

1925, and the centenary of lifeboat service in Appledore. This boat was the *'V.C.S.'*, the first motor lifeboat in the Bristol Channel, presented in 1922 at a cost of over £8,000. As she was bigger than previous boats, the boathouse had to be enlarged and the Badstep slip-way altered to accommodate her. She saved forty-one lives during her sixteen years of service. *(North Devon Museum Trust)*

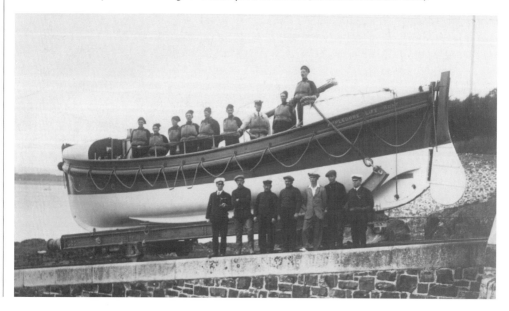

The *'Jane Hannah McDonald III'* lifeboat shown here on the Badstep slip-way in about 1920.
Among the crew were John Berry (Cox'n), Steven Bignell (2nd Cox'n) and Richard Berry (Bowman).
(North Devon Museum Trust)

The Appledore lifeboat *'Hope'*
seen here at the end of her
working life in 1890 after 28
years service. Her most
famous rescue was in 1868,
when her crew rescued 9 lives
from the Austrian barque
'Pace' which was wrecked on
Northam Burrows in a
tremendous gale. The
conditions were ferocious,
the *'Hope'* had her rudder
torn away, and the cox'n was
almost killed when trapped
between the lifeboat and the
wrecked ship. Despite this,
the crew valiantly braved the
conditions and got the
survivors to shore. For their
service, as well as being
awarded medals from the
RNLI, Joseph Cox (cox'n), his
son Joseph Cox, and John
Kelly were presented with
silver crosses of merit by the
Emperor of Austria.
(North Devon Museum Trust)

These pictures show the construction in an Appledore boat-yard of water-borne movable targets being made for the Royal Navy in 1912, to be used in practice firing exercises. *(North Devon Museum Trust)*

(North Devon Museum Trust)

Philip Kelly Harris was a well-known ship repairer of Appledore, but in 1909 he started building a schooner called the *'P T Harris'* in his New Quay yard. She was the last wooden cargo sailing vessel built on the Torridge, and is shown here under construction in 1910. She was launched in 1912, but tragedy struck her on a voyage in 1916, when she vanished without trace, and all the crew were lost. It was assumed that she fell victim to a German U-boat, but only her life-buoy was ever recovered, and is now in the Appledore Maritime Museum. *(North Devon Museum Trust)*

The crew of the *'P T Harris'* were the son of the owner: Thomas Harris (master) and two of his grandchildren: Thomas Leonard Harris (16) and William Ford Harris (14). The other men were Walter Lesslie and Ernest Parkhouse. They are all shown here in a poignant photo not long before the fateful voyage in which they all drowned. For Philip Kelly Harris to lose his son and two of his grandchildren was too much, and he never built another ship again. *(North Devon Museum Trust)*

The grave of Thomas's wife in the churchyard is also a memorial to her husband and two sons, and bears this poem as part of the inscription:

> WE CANNOT BEND BESIDE THEIR GRAVE,
> FOR THEY SLEEP IN THE SECRET SEA,
> AND NOT ONE GENTLE WHISPERING WAVE,
> WILL TELL THE PLACE TO ME:
> BUT THOUGH UNSEEN BY HUMAN EYE,
> THOUGH MORTALS KNOW IT NOT,
> THEIR FATHER KNOWETH WHERE THEY LIE,
> AND ANGELS GUARD THEIR SPOT.

William Yeo (1813-1872). It is perhaps inevitable that anyone who became (in modern terms) a multi-millionaire, did so at the expense of other people. In Appledore, if you crossed William Yeo, employment was denied to you, and many other difficulties likely to be put in your way to prevent you carrying on your trade. His nick-name was 'the black ram', and was based on the Appledore pronunciation of the name Yeo (ewe).
(Collingwood Yeo)

Richmond House, Appledore.

THIS EVENING, MONDAY JANUARY 3RD, 1859.

THE BIDEFORD & APPLEDORE DRAMATIC SOCIETY

Will have the pleasure of appearing for this Night only.

THE PERFORMANCE

TO COMMENCE WITH THE LAUGHABLE COMIDETTA IN ONE ACT, BY G. M. MORTON, Esq., entitled

Away with Melancholy

(By the Bideford Dramatic Society.)

CHARACTERS.

Mr. Windsor Brown, (a flighty young gentleman).............................Mr. W. Yelland.
Mr. Trimmer, (a remarkably cool gentleman)...............................Mr. R. E. Yelland.
David, (rather an eccentric Character, Windsor Brown's Servant)............Mr. Joce.
Mrs. Maynard, (a Widow, broke no end of hearts, and about to do for Windsor Brown) Miss E. Doidge.
Miss Kitty Cobb, (a dashing young Milliner)............................Miss Kate Doidge.
Dainty, a remarkably nice Servant ....Miss Tomlins.

Scene. ....A private Boarding House.

To conclude with a grand, new, original, whimsical, historical, logical, drollical, mystical new Christmas Pantomime entitled

Harlequin Puss in Boots.

HEY DIDDLE DIDDLE OR CHARITY rewarded.

Puss in Boots, (a Cat, though of small dimensions) of rather a romantic, and roving disposition fond of Wild Fowl................................Mr. C. Broad.
Florinet, A tolerably good natured fellow, though never satisfied, the delight of all romantic young ladies..Mr. Yelland, Jun.
The King (a fine old gent of the heavy School, partial to fast colours, and being Monarch of all, he surveys)...Mr. Yelland.
First and Second Lords of the Court.....................................Messrs. Williams.
The Ogre, (an horrid monster, Lady Killer Warranted to make a duck of a husband though never yet been induced to enter the bands of Hymen, partial to foreign travel) ....Mr. Pickard.
Herald,...Miss Bella Yeo.
Hatmakers...The Misses Yeo.
Fairy, Well I can't describe her, come and see her.......................Miss Polly Yeo
The Queen, (The Kings better half, a lover of Petticoat Government)...........Miss Yeo.
Princess, (Waiting but not in vain I hope, for some very nice young man; Pegtops indispensible) ....Miss Tomlins
Lady in Waiting, (also anxiously awaiting her time)........................Miss Kate Doidge.

For a correct account of Scenery and Effects the audience are particularly recommended to read the Child's Edition of Puss in Boots which can be obtained at Mr. BERRY'S, Mill Street, Bideford, PRICE ONE PENNY, the only correct Edition.

THE PERFORMANCE TO COMMENCE AT EIGHT O'CLOCK.

A poster for an evening of festive New Year entertainment to be held in William Yeo's house in 1859. The Bideford Dramatic Society appear to have been invited to perform in Richmond house, as long as William Yeo's daughters can also take part in the pantomime. Whilst Polly Yeo would have been ten at the time, Belle Yeo was just six years old, and probably stole the show!

The New Quay Dock shown on the right, was built by William Yeo, at about the same time as the Richmond Dock. The ketch *'Saidie R'* is shown being worked on here in 1931. In ship-building and repair yards such as this, the sound of plane and chisel, adze and mallet must have echoed everywhere when they were in full production. In the 1930s however, business was poor, and all the Appledore yards suffered. During World War II, wooden minesweepers were built in this yard, but it fell into disuse, and was eventually filled in, in 1973. *(National Maritime Museum, Greenwich, London)*

Richmond Dock in about 1960. Nicholas Pevsner in his Buildings of England, wrote about Appledore: "A little maritime settlement at the meeting of the Taw and Torridge estuaries, remarkably unspoilt, a welcome contrast to the indifferent seaside suburbia between Northam and Westward Ho! The shipbuilding industry which flourished especially in the 18th and 19th centuries as a result of the North American trade, miraculously still continues". *(North Devon Museum Trust)*

A portrait of Thomas Burnard Chanter, merchant, and Lord of the Manor of Northam (1797-1874), who in 1845 had the foresight to organise the building of the Quay at Appledore.
(Mrs Peter Cardew)

The elaborate tomb of Thomas Chanter and his wife Isabella in Northam churchyard. He maintained a great interest in local business and politics, until he died aged 76.

This engraving from 1830 shows Appledore from Instow, and includes below smaller engravings of the properties of Thomas Hogg esquire, a local landowner. Many of these properties were never built, and this tells us more of Thomas Hogg's intentions in terms of his place in the village, than of the historical accuracy of this picture. Note the bathing machines on Instow foreshore, and the slightly over-emphasised scale of Staddon Hill. *(North Devon Museum Trust)*

On the right is John Thomas Passmore, about 1905. Although living at Northam, he was the general carrier of goods to and from Appledore at this time. He lived in Cross Street, Northam, and kept his horse in a stable at the back of his house, but had to take it through the house each time, to get it out.
(North Devon Museum Trust)

The *'Royal George'* pub in Irsha Street in 1897, with the landlord William Kelly standing in the doorway. He used to brew his own beer on the premises, indeed the two upper right windows are actually painted dummies, behind which the brewing took place, obviously situated on the seaward side of the building so that the waste malt products could easily be discarded into he sea. No doubt his customers appreciated his efforts with beer at around 2d per pint. *(Courtesy: Royal George, Appledore)*

A book on the history of Appledore, would not be complete without including Hocking's ice-cream vans.
They started this business in 1936, and this is their first van, a converted 1929 Morris Cowley with
David Wood Hocking and his daughter Shirley seen here in about 1939.
(Kind permission: David & Geoffrey Hocking)

This annual outing by Appledore girls working in the Buckleigh laundry in about 1925, was arranged
through Hockings transport, who owned Ensign Garages and the char-a-banc pictured here.
In the picture are David Wood Hocking (driver), and among the girls in the front are Lillian Jeffery,
Sylvia Dummett, and Frances Bowden. Towards the back, in the white dress, is Beatrice Slade.
(Kind permission of Shirley Hocking)

The early 1930s at the top of the old slip-way, and a single car parked on the Quay signifies what is to come in terms of motor transport. The first few car owners in the village were Rev Scholey, Ernest Hocking, and William Lamey; however this Ford E-type belongs to Dr Valentine whose surgery is nearby. The two men talking together are Thomas Slade and Capt. Bartholomew (Batty) Lamey. The ship in the foreground is a ketch, curiously called 'Ketch'! *(North Devon Museum Trust)*

Whilst today's Baptist Sunday School is still going strong, it is unlikely to see quite as many children as this again. This march by the Sunday School children took place in 1933, and is seen here in Myrtle Street. The children holding the banner are Walter Tuplin (left) and Reg Carter (right). *(E R Carter)*

High tides which flood the Quay are not just a modern event. Many of the lower houses in Appledore had to put boards up at their doorways to keep out water at times like this, although not always successfully. This high spring tide in the 1930s almost looks as though the ketch 'Hobah' will be lifted over the quay wall, although in this picture it is difficult to see where the Quay edge is.

Beware any pedestrians at times like this. On one dark evening in the 1920s, a woman from West Appledore was served in the chemist shop on the Quay, and after leaving the shop she was never seen again. Kidnapping was hardly likely, and it was assumed that in the darkness she stumbled over the Quay edge, and was taken out to sea by the tide. As I said - pedestrians beware!
(National Maritime Museum, Greenwich, London)

Many houses in Appledore were built within the grasp of the sea, and it is therefore not surprising that occasionally the sea wins its battle. These are the remains of three cottages undermined and demolished, near the *'Royal George'* pub in Irsha Street, after a gale in December 1910. *(North Devon Museum Trust)*

The outside of St Mary's church seen from the north. The large tree in the foreground is no longer there, but the graves in this part of the churchyard remain largely unchanged. Note however that the church does not yet have a tower – this was built in 1908, some seventy years after the church was built.
You can see however, the small belfry on the back of the Nave, which housed a single bell to summon the faithful, until the tower, with its peal of eight bells was completed. *(National Monuments Record Centre)*

Below is the interior of the church after internal alterations had been carried out, and electric light installed in the 1930s. *(Courtesy: The Francis Frith Collection)*

The entrance to Appledore Vicarage seen in about 1910. It was built in 1897 but is now a residential home. During its former life it was home to the vicars of Appledore from the time of the Rev. Alfred Gurney Goldsmith. The first vicar of Appledore was Rev. Edward Reynolds, who held office until 1896, but he used Staddon House as the vicarage. *(North Devon Museum Trust)*

St Mary's church was built in 1838 on the site of a former chapel, supposedly Roman Catholic, and according to a directory of 1850, many old relics were found whilst digging the foundations for this church, although what these might have been is not recorded. In 1838 funds were not available to complete the tower, so this was added at a later date. The church design was by J Williams with bare pinnacles on the east end, and a large perpendicular window. The tower (when it was added in 1908) was by John Smith of Bideford, and the uncompleted base of it can just be seen on the left of the picture. *(North Devon County Record Office)*

This replica schooner shown below was constructed in the Appledore Bible Christian Chapel for a special occasion in about 1900. The schooner is the *'Gertrude'* and was owned by Philip Waters, who can be seen on the right of the picture. The others in the picture (right to left) are John Hopkins, Sydney Copp, Jack Carter and Robert Batten. The tall man on the left is Rev Dean. The Chapel, which was in Irsha Street, was demolished in 1907. *(E R Carter)*

Appledore Regatta in the 1920s. Regatta day in Appledore was one of the social highlights of the year, always held early August. The Quay would be filled with stalls and decorations, and crowds four or five deep watched the races on the front. Events included the 2-man and 4-man gig races, with teams from all over the West of England competing. There were also mixed crew races, sculling races, swimming races, gig and punt chase, miller and sweep battle, and of course the greasy pole. *(Maritime Trust)*

The class of 1908-09 at Appledore National School. The master on the left is Frederick Cole, but do you recognise anyone else here?

The village of Appledore from the south, this picture taken in the 1920s, showing clearly the Hubbastone Quarry, with Chanter's Folly perched on the very edge. *(Knights Photographers, Barnstaple)*

The ceremony that took place when laying the foundation stone for the Congregational Church manse (opposite Stony Lane at top of Richmond Hill) in 1909.
(Courtesy: United Reformed Church)

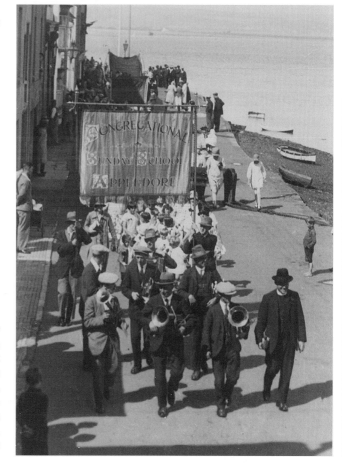

This procession along the Quay by the Congregational Church and their Sunday School took place in the late 1920s. The minister at the time was the Rev. A. C. Brockett who served from 1924 to 1939, and is seen here on the right of the picture.
(Courtesy: United Reformed Church)

Horse and cart transport has started to be replaced by motor transport, both seen here in this picture from about 1930. The men on the Quay are standing under one of the first electric street lights, watching a couple of trading smacks heading out to sea. *(Courtesy: The Francis Frith Collection)*

The picture below was issued as a postcard in 1964. The old gentleman sitting on the bench has a young boy with him, both watching the crabbing that is taking place, and the Instow ferry arriving. He is Ernest Carter enjoying a morning out with his nine-year-old grandson. Little did they realise that they were being immortalised on a postcard, or indeed that the boy would grow up to write a history of the village.

For a county often swept by high winds, Devon had remarkably few windmills. This was probably due to the availability of many suitable sites for water mills in more sheltered locations. However, this windmill graced the hills at Wooda behind Appledore for many centuries. It was indicated on maps of the 17th century, and survived until the early 20th century, when parts of it were considered dangerous and taken down. A violent storm in December 1920 completed its demise, and for some years afterwards large piles of debris lay surrounding it in the field.

(Devon & Cornwall Notes and Queries)

(Devon & Cornwall Notes and Queries)

(E R Carter)

Severe winters are rare in Appledore. This picture taken in 1963 however, shows the after effects of extreme low temperatures that froze the river, and washed large blocks of ice downstream.

(North Devon Museum Trust)

This is the workforce of the P K Harris yard in 1906. The majority of their work involved ship repairs, but they also built the ill-fated schooner '*P T Harris*' a few years later. Philip Kelly Harris is third from the left on the front row.

A small racing gig under construction in John Hinks yard in 1920.
(North Devon Museum Trust Collections)

The Richmond dry-dock with two vessels in tandem undergoing repairs. The entrance to the dock was not protected by dock gates, but by a caisson, or 'ga-zoon' as the locals often called it. The large sail loft buildings on the right of the picture were demolished after a fire gutted them in 1947.
(North Devon Museum Trust)

The newly completed promenade shown below was constructed on the land below St Mary's church in about 1940. The road leading around the lower end of the church was also created at this time.
(Courtesy: The Francis Frith Collection)

The entrance to the Richmond Dock in the early 1950s.
Eric Delderfield writing at exactly this time said that *"Appledore is different from the usual seaport of this type, for the past not only lingers but is linked with the present by its shipping activities. True, they are on a smaller scale, for but one large boatbuilding concern remains, although there are dozens of smaller ones, but the Appledore tradition of hundreds of years of seamen and craft is carried on".*
(Courtesy: The Francis Frith Collection)

A German timber trading boat visiting Appledore during the 1930s shows the type of cargoes that were being brought into this port at the time. The date is shortly before the 2nd World War, so note the swastika flag flying freely on the bow of the vessel. *(North Devon Museum Trust Collections)*

The south end of Appledore Quay during the Second World War, taken from the deck of a landing craft. Note the small harbour office built on the corner to monitor shipping during this period. Chanter's Folly is prominent on the hill in the distance. *(North Devon Museum Trust)*

This picture was taken in 1940, showing work started on the construction of the new Quay.
Work was started in 1939, then stopped on the outbreak of war, and then started again as part of the war
effort. This picture appears to show work stopped, but these children still seem to find it interesting.
It clearly shows how much additional space was created by the Quay being extended from its former
curved line (which followed the line of the quay-front buildings), into the straight efficient frontage
taking shape here.*(North Devon Museum Trust Collections)*

Work being carried out at the north end of Appledore Quay, to complete its construction in about 1940.
Certainly a hive of activity, with temporary track-ways laid to assist the movement of large quantities of
material, but most of the work appears to be done by hand. The line of the old slip-way at this point is
being used to bring materials up to the Quay level. *(North Devon Museum Trust Collections)*

1944, and wartime in Appledore. This picture shows just a small number of the troops that were stationed there and at Instow during the 2nd World War. Much training and many exercises were carried out in preparation for the 'D Day' landings, and which no doubt contributed greatly to the success of this campaign. *(North Devon Museum Trust Collections)*

On the river, many new ideas were being tried, and much testing and training was carried out on amphibious craft and vehicles. This continued on after the end of the War, with this picture showing a Land Rover disembarking from a landing craft onto the sands at Instow.
(North Devon Museum Trust Collections)

This view of Appledore shows that landing craft were still around in the 1960s, training on the beachfront at Instow.

The original Roll of Honour board in St Mary's churchyard, before the War Memorial was set up in the open space just outside the gates.
(North Devon Museum Trust)

This ship, one of the old 'wooden walls of England', was brought to Appledore in 1924 at the end of her life, and was broken up at Hinks' ship-breaking yard. Commonly known as the 'Revenge', her real name was the 'Empress', and she created a magnificent sight in the Torridge for the time she was there. She had a magnificent history, having fought closely at the Battle of Trafalgar, fighting off two ships simultaneously. Parts of her still exist in the area, as many of her timbers were used in building work taking place in Appledore and Northam at the time. *(North Devon Museum Trust)*

A ships graveyard. Occasionally ships were broken up officially, but often they were just left on the riverbank to rot when they had reached the end of their useful life. These ships in Hinks yard are waiting to be broken up. *(North Devon Museum Trust)*

The picture above is of the schooner '*M A James*' in 1950 lying where she was left on the beach at Boathyde after the 2nd World War. Fifty years on, and the view below shows that in the intervening period much decay has occured, and eventually she will disappear altogether. *(North Devon Museum Trust Collections)*

Two atmospheric pictures taken of the beach below Irsha Street by John Beara. This was the playground for many small boys, and working area for fishermen, many of whose boats can be seen here.
(North Devon Museum Trust)

(North Devon Museum Trust)

View of East Appledore from half-way up Staddon Hill looking up the river. The picture above was
taken in 1923; Chanter's Folly can be seen in the distance, but the houses on the Tomouth estate
have not been built. The house in the centre with a curved window arch is now the Maritime Museum in
Odun Road. The same view today (below) looks little different, apart from the obvious new development.
(National Maritime Museum, Greenwich, London)

CHAPTER TWO

SLADE
Family History

THE PICTURES INCLUDED IN THIS BOOK showing Appledore in times past give an excellent idea of what the village was like in those days. To really make the history of a village come alive however, it is best illustrated by telling the story of the people who lived in it, what they did in their lives, how they earned their living, the calamities that overcame them, and the happier times between. It can be particularly interesting if their history was well documented in some way, and can be carefully researched to reveal a story that has previously been untold. This is unlikely to be the case for the average village residents one-hundred to two-hundred years ago, as most inland villages were dependant on an agricultural economy, and the population spent most of their time working on the land growing their own food, and living very rural lives. Whilst the occasional legal document relating the title of land can show some interesting facts about who owned what, it is difficult to build a story of people's lives from this, in the absence of any other information.

Luckily, Appledore is not such a village. It has been a thriving port for many centuries, and the local economy is based almost entirely on shipbuilding and seafaring. If the economy had been based on fishing, then this would have had similarities to an agricultural economy (farming the sea not the land), and recorded events in fishing would probably be just as difficult to make a story from as from farming. But because Appledore's wealth and

interest is in seafaring, the history of ships and voyages is well recorded, which when adding the names of the people who took part in it, can be used to greater effect to build a story that can be illustrated and brought to life.

It would be impossible to tell the story of all the families in the village in this one book, so I have limited it to just one family - the **Slade** family. Although probably not the most prominent family in the village, they certainly had an interesting history, starting firstly as newcomers to the village, then employed as seafarers, then as captains of trading vessels, and subsequently as owners of the vessels themselves. They forged for themselves a successful business, eventually becoming moderately wealthy by the time that the coasting trade had died out around the time of the Second World War, indeed they have been described as one of the most successful family ship owning businesses in the south-west of England. Over the period from about 1890 up to the Second World War, the Slade family owned and ran some twenty-two various vessels at different times, and became successful and prosperous in this trade. Three members particularly made a success in this business (Thomas, Richard and William), but what hasn't been acknowledged before is that the process of owning and managing these vessels was all started by a woman . . . . .

Mary ann Slade

MARY ANN SLADE was born in Appledore in 1856, the eldest daughter of **Thomas** and **Elizabeth Slade**. Her father was already a seasoned mariner having made many voyages including at least eight to Quebec. Thomas and Elizabeth met and married in Bristol, as Elizabeth was in service there as a ladies maid, although she was an Appledore girl. After they were married in December 1854, they returned to live in Appledore in time for Mary Ann to be born in April 1856.

Mary Ann grew up in Irsha Street as the eldest of eleven children, and after leaving school spent some time in Bristol among her mother's friends where she learned the trade of dressmaking. She returned to Appledore, and when she was twenty-four she married an Appledore seaman named George Quance, who was two months older than Mary Ann, and had been brought up in New Street at the other end of the village. It is likely that Mary Ann had known him throughout their childhood and she obviously recognised in him

someone who could work hard and earn money to keep the family.

In his adult life, George became a seafarer firstly on local trading vessels, and then travelling further afield several times to China on the tea clippers, but after their marriage, he worked on coastal schooners with Mary's brother William. After this he became mate on a brigantine, and then master of a little coastal schooner trading mostly onto the Cornish beaches and in the Bristol Channel area, usually with cargoes of coal. Whether George would also have made a good father would never be known, as they were not to be blessed with any children.

Mary Ann was determined to make something of herself though, and worked as a dressmaker to bring in income for the family. She would spend all day in her customers' houses working with her sewing machine, or sometimes in her own home in Irsha Street all night to complete her orders. In this way she earned enough to run the house, and any

money which her husband brought home was put aside, unknown to George who was apparently rather wild with his companions and didn't care much about money matters.

By 1888 therefore Mary Ann had saved up a fairly large sum of money. She obviously thought the world of George and had immense trust in

his abilities, so decided to reward him, and arranged to buy outright a small ketch for her husband. One day when he had come home for lunch after some drinks with his fellow seamen, Mary Ann said to him *'There's something that I'm going to do for you if you promise to back me up in every way. I've got the money to buy you a little vessel of your own so that you'll be independent of everybody'*. George was apparently speechless when she told him this, and had obviously underestimated his wife's capabilities and determination. He thought about it, and the next day looked over his new vessel, and finally promised her that if the vessel was bought for him, then he would see that it made money for them.

The vessel that Mary Ann bought was the *'Nouvelle Marie'*, a sturdy ketch of some forty-nine tons, built in France twenty years earlier, and which was then owned by a trader from County Cork in Southern Ireland.

George was determined to show Mary Ann he was worth her confidence in him, and worked hard with the *'Nouvelle Marie'*, mostly

in the coal trade from South Wales. In fact it is recorded that he once discharged three cargoes of coal in the Bristol Channel area within a week, a record which has never been equalled by a sailing vessel.

And so started the family business of owning and running vessels.

THE STORY OF THE *NOUVELLE MARIE*

A TYPICAL series of voyages for the *'Nouvelle Marie'* is recorded in the surviving documents for 1895, and shows George Quance with a crew of two, making four trips to Bristol & Gloucester, six to Newport, seven to Lydney, and eight to Cornish ports like Falmouth, Gorran Haven, Fowey and Newquay. In between all of these, Appledore was visited eight times, so the amount of time spent at home with Mary Ann would only have been a small proportion of the year, and therefore awaited eagerly by both George and Mary Ann.

As hard as George worked with the *'Nouvelle Marie'*, by all accounts so did Mary Ann with her dressmaking. Indeed after not much more time had passed, she had put by enough money to buy their own house in Irsha Street, and subsequently one or two other houses which were rented out to other families.

The crew list document for the first voyages of the 'Nouvelle Marie' after Mary Ann obtained the boat for George Quance in 1888. Documents such as these are valuable in tracing the history of a vessel, and her voyages. This one tells us that the crew were: George Quance (master, 32), Philip Hutchings (mate, 20), William Lewis (seaman, 20) and Albert Cawsey (seaman, 18). Cargo carrying voyages were made to Lydney, Newport, St Ives, and other small Cornish beaches. (Public Record Office - BT99/1611)

By 1909, George had also acquired other vessels; and the *'Nouvelle Marie'* was being run under the control of a hired master and crew:

- Captain **Joshua Boon** (64) master
- his son **William Boon** (24) mate
- and his nephew **William Cobbledick** (17) able seaman,

when a tragedy occurred that affected not only the Slade & Quance families, but also the whole village of Appledore.

IN MARCH 1909 the vessel had left Newport in fine weather laden with coal bound for Bude, but by the time they got to Bideford Bay, a storm had blown up from the south-west, and they were unable to get around Hartland Point, so anchored off Clovelly to weather out the gale. They stayed there until the following day, but the storm had not abated, and the conditions were unsafe for a vessel to cross the bar into the Torridge estuary. The captain decided to run back up the Bristol Channel to seek shelter, and another vessel (the *'Mabel'*) who was also with her, managed to get into Ilfracombe, but the *'Nouvelle Marie'* overshot the mark, and was blown further up the Bristol Channel. What happened next is unknown, but they must have lost their position in the worsening storm, and been unable to control or navigate the vessel properly. The boat was found wrecked the next morning on rocks near Barry in South Wales, as the local paper subsequently described:......

"A gloom was cast over the town of Appledore on Thursday evening by the receipt of the news that the ketch 'Nouvelle Marie' of Appledore, had been washed ashore near Barry a total

wreck, and that nothing was seen or known of the crew, who it is feared had been drowned. The crew consisted of Appledore men.....Captain J Boon was about 65 years of age, his son William Boon about 22, and his nephew William Cobbledick about 16. Very pathetic scenes were witnessed when the relatives heard of the disaster.....it is many years ago that such a calamity has come to Appledore.....flags are being flown at half-mast as a mark of respect."
Bideford & North Devon Weekly Gazette, 30th March 1909

"The vessel was seen in the bay from Appledore, and recognised as a home craft. It was then blowing a heavy gale from the SW, and it is thought that the Captain not being able to weather Hartland Point made up-channel for shelter. The body of the man Cobbledick was picked up on Sunday night at Barry, and the police communicated by telephone with Appledore. On Monday morning Mr J Cawsey went to identify the body."
North Devon Journal, 1st April 1909

The Captain and crew were well known to Mary Ann and George, as they lived nearby in Irsha Street, so the tragedy of losing three friends was compounded by the loss of their first vessel that had served them so well. It must have been heartbreaking to have heard the news of the disaster, and the community spirit of Appledore pulled together to comfort and support the families in their bereavement. The recovery of the three bodies and the subsequent funerals were also reported:......

"At Barry on Tuesday last, John Cawsey, master mariner of Appledore identified the body of the deceased as that of his nephew. The features were recognisable, and the initials 'W.C.' were worked on the deceased's guernsey, and tattooed on his arm. The jersey and shirt worn by the deceased were found on the head, as if he had made an attempt to divest himself of

those garments whilst in the water."
Barry Dock News, 2nd April 1909

"On Friday afternoon, the funeral of William Cobbledick who was drowned at Barry from the ketch 'Nouvelle Marie' took place amid many signs of public sympathy in St Mary's churchyard..... A jersey belonging to the young man Boon has been washed ashore inside out (which shows it was pulled off in a hurry). Some think that the lad Cobbledick got ashore alive, and died from exposure, whilst other theories are that the young man Boon was known to be a splendid swimmer, and it is thought that he took the lad ashore first, and then went to assist his father, the result being that all perished. This is of course all supposition, and the real facts will never be known, but as the young Boon was an expert swimmer, a great deal of credit is attributed to this version in the town."
Bideford & North Devon Weekly Gazette, 6th April 1909

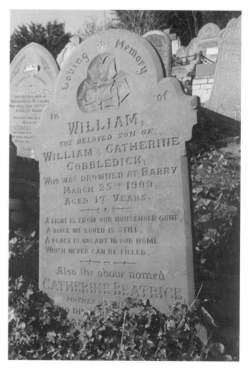

The grave of William Cobbledick in Appledore churchyard.

Over two weeks later, the recovery of the body of the vessel's master: Captain Joshua Boon was reported. This was approximately two miles east of where the 'Nouvelle Marie' was wrecked......

"The body of a man picked up on Monday last in the channel off Nell's Point, Barry is identified as that of Captain Joshua Boon, who with two other members of the crew was drowned when the ketch 'Nouvelle Marie' was driven ashore and wrecked off Porthkerry during the gale a fortnight ago.... The Captain's remains were in an advanced state of decomposition, and were removed to the mortuary to await the coroner's inquiry."

Barry Dock News, 16th April 1909

The remains of Captain Boon were conveyed to Appledore on 14th April by the steamer 'Eddy', and buried in St Mary's churchyard two days later. The local paper reported that the Captain's widow was too ill and prostrate to attend the funeral. The body of her son had still to be recovered, and it was another six weeks before the South Wales paper reported the following......

"On Wednesday evening, a body apparently that of a young seaman, was washed ashore at Llantwit Major. The remains were in an advanced state of decomposition with the head and right arm missing, and believed to be those of the young man Boon, of Appledore, a member of the ketch 'Nouvelle Marie' which foundered in a gale off Barry about three months ago."

Barry Dock News, 28th May 1909

This body was subsequently identified at the inquest at Llantwit Major, and brought to Appledore for burial with his father. The grave can still be seen in Appledore churchyard engraved with the emblem of an anchor.

THIS MAY WELL have been the end of this tragic tale, had it not been for a recent Act of Parliament - the 'Workmen's Compensation

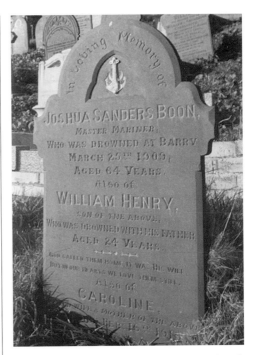

The grave of Joshua Boon in Appledore churchyard.

Act 1906'. This made it possible for employees involved in accidents to be compensated for loss of earnings (or in this case for their dependants to receive compensation). The 'Nouvelle Marie' was insured by Mary Ann with the Ship Owners Mutual Insurance Association of Braunton, and this insurance also covered the vessel's master and crew against accident. Captain Joshua Boon's widow Charlotte therefore claimed compensation for her husband's loss of earnings, and on behalf of the rest of the crew, which she was entitled to do under the Act.

The case came to court in October 1909 in Bideford, and a legal battle followed:......

"An important point under the Workmen's Compensation Act as affecting the position of captains working vessels under the 'thirds' system, came before his Honour Judge Beresford at Bideford County Court on Wednesday. The Court was crowded, a large number of Appledore and seafaring men being present,

and great interest being manifested in the action.

Charlotte Boon's solicitor contended that the applicant's case was supported by the respondents insurance of the Captain. The fact that an owner insures the Captain and crew showed that she considered the men were her servants. The owner was liable in law for the wages, although she did not engage the crew, but could be sued for them in default of the Captain paying them. This was a very important case because if his Honour were to find the owner was not responsible then so far as these vessels were concerned the Workman's Compensation Act was null and void.

After 3 hours of legal argument, and witnesses' accounts of the events leading up to, and after the accident, Judge Beresford in giving judgement said.....it was quite clear to his mind that the relationship of master and servant did exist.....and the applicants were entitled to recover, and he gave judgement in their favour."

Bideford & North Devon Weekly Gazette, 26th Nov 1909

This result was received with satisfaction by the people attending the court, and everyone came away satisfied that the judgement had been correct.

However the Insurance Company was presumably pressured to submit an appeal. They may have felt that the possibility of having this decision reversed was likely to succeed, as the legislation was new and untested. Therefore, a month after the original case, an appeal was heard at the Divisional Court, presided over by the Master of the Rolls himself, because of the importance of this case. The result was an overturning of the previous judgement, as it was determined that Captain Joshua Boon was NOT a servant of Mary Ann under the terms of the Act, because it was shown that there were no restrictions in force that would normally be placed upon a servant.

"Now the evidence....seems to be quite clear, and is really uncontradicted. The ship owner Mrs Quance finds the vessel, finds the gear and tackle, she does not engage the men. For that purpose....she 'intrusts' the ketch to a master, in this case Captain Boon. It is for him....to go to what port he likes, to engage what crew he likes and to pay what wages he likes. His only obligation is to pay to Mrs Quance one third of the gross freight that may be earned. Out of the balance he pays his crew, pays any dues and expenses. In those circumstances, what is there to suggest the relation of master and servant? It follows therefore, the award must be made in favour of the appellant."

The Law Times, 28th May 1910

The result of this appeal that overturned the previous judgement stunned Charlotte Boon and the other dependants of the 'Nouvelle Marie's' crew, and as you can imagine, the other local seafarers were up in arms about this decision. The seafaring community was in uproar about not only the injustice of it, but the consequences for the future of sailing under the same system of insurance and responsibilities.

It had the effect of nearly wrecking the share sailing system, and the whole structure of local ship owning and operation in the Bristol Channel area. A general stoppage was threatened, which in turn threatened employment in the dockyards. The insurance clubs were eventually forced to take the matter up with the London clubs, who, as they would be faced with a boycott from the people who normally provided their wealth and business, were left with little choice but to agree to be responsible for all future claims. Despite the interpretation of the Compensation Act, they gave in, and a victory was eventually had by the ship masters and owners.

A triumph of common sense, which regrettably the relatives of the 'Nouvelle Marie's' crew were unable to take advantage of, as it was saddening to discover that they were never compensated for their loss.

GEORGE AND MARY ANN QUANCE

AFTER THIS TERRIBLE tragedy, what did the future have in store for George and Mary Ann? By this time, they had made sufficient money to have invested in various other vessels:

- **'Elizabeth Jane'**, (of which more later),
- **'Ulelia'**, a fifty-eight ton ketch built in Truro in 1877 (which was partly owned with Mary Ann's brother William Kingdon Slade),
- **'Alpha'**, a sister ship to the *'Ulelia'*, which was proved to be very fast in competition, and run after George's death by William Kingdon Slade until sold in 1912. and
- **'J.W.V.'** (a fifty-eight ton schooner).

The *'J.W.V.'* was built in South Cornwall in 1871, and bought by George Quance in 1903. Unfortunately, this vessel was run down by a dredger in Southampton Water less than two weeks before the *'Nouvelle Marie'* disaster, and was sunk with its cargo of scrap steel. Fortunately on this occasion, the crew:

- Captain **William Jillings**
- **James Taylor**
- **Frank Down**
- and **J Jillings** (son of the captain)

who were all Appledore men, were picked up from the water with nothing more than a good soaking to show for the experience, and were able to travel back home to Appledore on the train. These men were much luckier than the *'Nouvelle Marie's'* crew, and lived to sail again. A subsequent court case against the owners of the dredger awarded all costs to George and Mary Ann, but the effect of losing two vessels within as many weeks must have taken a hard toll on them, and it is likely that they never really recovered from the shock of these two tragic accidents.

The following year (1910) Mary Ann died of cancer at the age of fifty-four. She had achieved so much in her life, and her true Appledore grit and determination will always be remembered by those who knew her, and those who have heard of what she had achieved. Without her initiative in purchasing the first vessel for the family, who knows how differently things might have turned out. The family obviously felt a great loss, and George must have missed her tremendously. After her death, he moved in with his cousin in Hillcliff Terrace at the end of Irsha Street, and being at a loose end, was persuaded by the local Baptist minister to take a Sunday School class. Apparently he didn't teach them much about the Bible; after reading them a chapter, he'd start telling his old sea yarns, although no doubt greatly exaggerated, and in the end, the

An oil painting of the ketch 'J.W.V.', by George Quance in 1906, after his retirement from the sea. Although not a quality painting, it has the great advantage of being absolutely accurate in terms of its depiction of the vessel and her rigging. (Private Collection)

boys wouldn't go to Sunday School unless 'Captain Quance' taught them; and by all accounts, he was a good story teller.

The following story of his was one of the favourites in Appledore:

"It was the rule in the 1890s for an Appledore boy to get half wages when he could furl the topsail at sea in all weathers. Uncle George was on his way home to lunch one day when he was stopped by the mother of the boy who sailed with him in the 'Nouvelle Marie'. She said, 'My boy Sammy is a big boy now and should have half wages.' 'Well,' said Uncle George, 'the rule is, as you know, the gaff topsail has to be taken in.' 'Oh', she said, 'my Sammy has been doing that for years.' Eventually the 'Nouvelle Marie' sailed, and sure enough the gaff topsail had to be furled off Hartland Point.

'Up you go Sammy,' says Uncle George, and up Sammy went. He only got about six or seven feet up when his legs started to shake and he had to come down again. Uncle George said, 'Why are your legs shaking Sammy?' 'It wasn't my legs shaking,' said Sammy, 'it was the wind blowing up the legs of my trousers, and if the old b**** wants half wages she can come here and let the wind blow up the legs of her trousers and see how she likes it!"
The Merchant Schooners: Basil Greenhill

George also spent time in retirement making models of ships and doing oil paintings of the vessels he had owned and admired in his working life. First he painted the *'Alpha'* (a sister ketch of the *'Ulelia'*, owned by William Kingdon Slade), then he produced increasingly better paintings showing the

The ketch 'Ulelia', painted here by George Quance, and owned jointly by William Kingdon Slade and George Quance from 1899 to 1916. She was wrecked in April 1930 on rocks in Southern Ireland, whilst under the control of Appledore Captain: James Reveley. (Private Collection)

'Nouvelle Marie', the 'J.W.V.' and the 'Ulelia'. These paintings may not be of great artistic quality, but they have a rugged splendour about them, having been painted by someone who knew the boats intimately. It can therefore be guaranteed that all of the technical details were absolutely correct in the pictures, so much so, that historians can today use them as primary sources of information about these lost vessels, and how they were rigged and sailed.

George, who was no doubt looking forward to a long and rewarding retirement, also passed the time taking visitors on short boat trips up the river Torridge, as no doubt did other retired sailors. However less than twelve months after Mary Ann died, another tragedy was to strike as he took some visitors from Bristol, a Miss Sarah Brunt and her

nephew and niece, on a boat trip up the river Torridge from Appledore. The visitors were staying in Appledore on holiday, and had taken the opportunity of the fine weather to take a trip on a sailing boat, when a sudden squall hit them . . .

"All seems to have gone well, until the boat was off Lower Cleavehouses. Here the craft seems to have been struck with a sudden puff of wind and sank in about five feet of water, the occupants being all thrown out. It was just after high tide, and the water was flowing down the river. The Instow sailing boat was the first to reach the place where the accident had happened and found Miss Brunt and her niece in the water supporting themselves with a paddle. Quance, who had been seen, and was believed to have been swimming, was found

nearly half a mile down the river. He was then floating on his face, his back apparently kept uppermost by the air in his clothes. He was taken into the boat and got ashore but was apparently dead when taken from the water. Every search was made, but nothing was seen of the boy until some hours afterwards, when the body was recovered from under the boat."

North Devon Journal, 5th Sept 1911

An inexplicable accident, the consequences of which were that two lives had been lost in conditions which appeared to be excellent for sailing, and within fifty yards of the river-bank. Notwithstanding the unnecessary loss of life of a fourteen year old boy, it is deeply ironic that a seasoned sailor, who had travelled the world should lose his life in the river within sight of his home, and which he must have known so well. George was apparently an excellent swimmer, unlike so many of his fellow seafarers, which makes the accident all the more mysterious, and it was felt that he had probably had a heart attack in the water for him not to have survived and saved the others. Captain Quance was described by his fellow sailors as a very steady, sober and capable man to have been in charge of this boat, and no-one that knew him would have hesitated to sail with him. He was widely known and respected in the coastal shipping trade, and was the local agent of the Braunton Shipping Insurance Club, and also a deacon of the Baptist Chapel. When news of the accident reached Appledore hundreds of people lined the Quay awaiting the arrival of the boat with his body. At his funeral a few days later, the rostrum was draped in black, there was an exceedingly large attendance of sailors, tradesmen and friends, and the blinds of the houses were drawn as a mark of respect, along the route of the cortege.

He was buried with Mary Ann in Appledore Churchyard under an imposing granite gravestone. Although George was part of a large family, in his will he asked for his estate to be divided among Mary Ann's brothers and sisters instead of his own. We do not know the reason for this, but it would be nice to think that he was still trying to repay the debt to Mary Ann for her trust in him in the early days when she worked so hard to buy him that first boat. George and Mary Ann's contribution to the subsequent success of the Slade family will however not be forgotten, and the little ketch 'Nouvelle Marie' which helped bring this about, and which had such a tragic end, will always have a special place in the memory of the Slade family.

The grave of George and Mary Ann Quance, in Appledore churchyard.

THE SLADE ANCESTRY

MARY ANN SLADE certainly appeared to have had a strong will and personality, and by all accounts it seems to have been a family trait, so presumably she must have inherited it from her ancestors. It would therefore be interesting to see what can be found out about them.

Up until recent generations, the name 'Slade' was in fact 'Slader', but the 'R' seems to have been dropped in the early 19th century, although some branches of the family still retain this version of the surname. Population movement in earlier centuries was very small, and in some villages virtually unknown. Appledore surnames can be traced back for centuries, with the same names occurring in documents from the 17th and 18th centuries as exist in the village today. In recent decades however population movement has increased dramatically, as the traditional trades associated with the village (seafaring and fishing) have declined to the point where alternative employment had to be sought elsewhere. Conversely, in recent years 'new blood' has repopulated the village, swelling it to the size it is today, and new surnames are now so plentiful, that the older names have become swamped. The modern village dweller's ability to travel means that more people can live in what many consider to be the most scenic village in the area, and still travel ten, twenty or more miles to work daily, thereby having the best of both worlds.

It was not the same two hundred and fifty years ago. The ability to travel widely was not possible, especially if you did not have the means, although Appledore people probably had more means than most. They had easy access to the sea, and the potential to visit other coastal or even foreign places, and sometimes even settle there. In the 18th and 19th centuries the trade across the Atlantic to the Eastern United States, Newfoundland and Prince Edward Island was huge, and this is reflected in some of the familiar local place names being re-created in these parts:

Biddeford (Maine), Barnstable (Massachusetts), Dartmouth (Nova Scotia), and no less than ten Plymouths scattered across various parts of the U.S.A. More significantly for us, the largest of the Isles of Shoals (seven miles off the coast of Maine) is called '*Appledore*', which seems to betray a visit by some enterprising Devonian at some time in the past, although who it might have been, has not been determined. Similarly, other New World place-names found their way back across the Atlantic; we have a '*Newfoundland Bay*' near Dartmouth, and in Appledore itself there is the '*Richmond Dock*', whose name came from Richmond Bay in Prince Edward Island.

THE SLADES OF APPLEDORE

TRACING THE SURNAMES back through the years has shown that the Slade family settled in Appledore comparatively recently. It was in the year 1777 that William Slade (actually Slader), who was born in North Molton about twenty miles away, decided to break with his family's tradition of farming, and move to Appledore in search of a better life at sea. Or perhaps it was the love of a local woman: Catherine Branton that persuaded him to move to the area, and then finding that the only work to be had in Appledore was to be a seaman. We will never know, but it cannot have been a totally unknown move, as five years prior to this, William's eldest brother John also moved to the area and married Catherine's younger sister Elizabeth. There began the start of a new Slade family history in Appledore.

The Slade ancestry can be traced back to the beginning of parish records in the village of North Molton:

John Slader
Born: c.1499 North Molton
|
Richard Slader
Born: 1525 North Molton
|
Thomas Slader = Agnes
Born: 1547 North Molton
|
Thomas Slader = Elizabeth
Born: 1582 North Molton
|
Michael Slader = Margaret Goulde
Born: 1602 North Molton
|
Michael Slader = Elinor Beale
Born: 1640 North Molton
|
Michael Slader = Joane Badcock
Born: 1668 North Molton
|
John Slader = Mary Squire
Born: 1694 North Molton
|
William Slader = Honor Nicholls
Born: 1724 North Molton
|
William Slader = Catherine Branton (of Bideford)
Born: 1756 North Molton
|
Thomas Harris Slader = Nancy Short
Born: 1783 Appledore
|
Thomas Harris (Parson) Slade = Susanna Smallridge
Born: 1810 Appledore
|
Thomas Slade = Elizabeth Kingdon
Born: 1833 Appledore
|
William Kingdon Slade = Rosina Annie Harding
Born: 1865 Appledore
|
Mary Elizabeth Slade = Ernest Carter
Born: 1898 Appledore

Appledore in the 18ᵗʰ century was certainly well established as a place of shipbuilding and seafaring, and there was presumably work aplenty for **William Slader** and his new wife Catherine. They had one girl and four boys, one of whom was **Thomas Harris Slader**, who became a rope-maker, and when married also had one girl and four boys. One of his sons (also called **Thomas Harris Slader**) had the nickname of '**Parson Slade**', not because he was a minister, but because he could read (a rare talent in those days), and therefore he always read the lesson in the local Bible Christian Chapel. He may also have done some preaching, we don't know. He does seem to have been keen to recreate the twelve disciples though, as he had twelve children, ten of which survived infancy, and yes, he was a carpenter by trade!

The start of the Slade story really begins with Parson Slade's son **Thomas Slade**. He was born on Christmas Day 1833, the second son of Parson Slade, and presumably grew up having little choice but to make a life for himself at sea. No photographs exist from this time so we have no idea what Thomas Slade looked like, however we do have a description of him which was recorded on his mariners ticket application in 1848, as follows…

Ticket no:	205,503
Issued:	Bideford 08 Nov 1848
Age:	14
Capacity:	Boy
Hair:	Red
Eyes:	Grey
Complexion:	Muddy
Height:	Growing

From the Crew List Documents in the Public Record Office, it is possible to reconstruct Thomas's career and voyages fairly accurately . . .

1849

Joined the crew of the schooner '*Industry*', as a fifteen year old ship's boy, engaged in the coasting trade from Bideford.

Later that year Thomas joined another schooner called the '*Alliance*'. She was a fifty-eight ton vessel also engaged in the local coasting trade; voyages were made to Newport, Plymouth, Porthcawl, and Neath. He left this vessel at the end of the year.

1850

In 1850, Thomas joined a forty-one ton brigantine called the '*Hazard*' which was

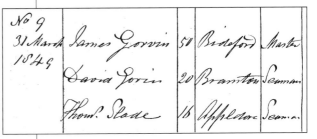

(Public Record Office)

trading between Cardiff and Bideford carrying limestone. As Thomas has now turned sixteen, he is no longer a ship's boy, and now becomes a seaman (*see document above*).

Later that year in September, he joined another vessel, this time a thirty-one ton ketch, grandly called the '*Queen Victoria*'.

1851

Thomas left the '*Queen Victoria*' on the 12th March, and presumably felt that it was now time to see something more of the world by joining an ocean going vessel, or maybe it was just because the pay was better.

He signed on with a tall square rigged ship of nine-hundred and fifty tons, called the '*Viceroy*' of London, as she was trading across the Atlantic to Quebec. No details of this vessel's voyages exist for this year, but it is likely that she made two crossings to Quebec.

1852

Thomas is now eighteen, and has become an 'ordinary seaman' with the rate of pay of £2 per month. He joins a smaller vessel, a barque called the 'Secret', which also sails to Quebec this year, from 5th April to 22 June, a round trip of eleven weeks. At the end of the voyage the master assessed Thomas's performance as being:

Cleanliness:	Good
Seamanship:	Medium
Conduct:	Very good

1853

Thomas's exact voyages this year are unknown, but we know that he served on a barque called the 'Solway' registered at Gloucester. This was a ship of some six-hundred tons built at New Brunswick, and which had recently traded to New Orleans, but whether Thomas actually went there we have been unable to discover. He left the vessel the following year in February at Cardiff.

DURING THIS TIME, Thomas must have spent some time in Bristol, as many of the vessels he had been serving on sailed from this large port, and it was perhaps a good place to try and make your fortune in the seafaring trade in the mid 19th century. Whilst he was in Bristol, Thomas must have met a young lady from Appledore called Elizabeth Kingdon, who was eighteen, and employed in Clifton as a lady's maid. Being from the same village, and a long way from home, they probably had something in common, and by all accounts got to know each other fairly well, and eventually fell in love.

Although we cannot prove it, it is said that at one time Thomas (being in Appledore) was unable to afford any transport to Bristol to see Elizabeth, and so walked all the way from

North Devon to see her - a romantic story that may well be based on some fact.

1854

On 1st March this year, Thomas joined the 'Ocean Queen', a one-thousand ton vessel sailing from Bristol carrying passengers across to Quebec.

(A voyage of this vessel in 1862 is commemorated in a slip-ware jug made at Barnstaple, and which is now one of the prize exhibits in the Appledore Maritime Museum).

Our Thomas made one voyage in the 'Ocean Queen' in 1854, arriving back in Bristol on 8th August where he had a two-week stop-over, and this must have enabled marriage to be suggested to Elizabeth. However, Thomas was soon to be off travelling again, and left on the 22nd August on an even larger vessel called the 'Princess Royal'. She was under the control of a master from Appledore, called James Scott, and sailed to Quebec returning on the 5th December.

DIRECT FROM BRISTOL.
FIRST SPRING SHIP FOR QUEBEC,
The fine Ship
OCEAN QUEEN,
CHARLES HOWES, COMMANDER,
1000 Tons Burthen.
Has room for Goods, and will take a limited number of Cabin and Steerage Passengers. She is intended to sail the first fair wind after the 25th March next.
For freight and Passage apply to
MARK WHITWILL, & SON,
Middle Avenue, Queen Square, and Grove.
Bristol, 24th Feb. 1854.

(Bristol Gazette and Advertiser)

Elizabeth must have been eagerly awaiting the return of Thomas, and probably wouldn't know when (or if) he would return until his ship docked in port. Their wedding must have been agreed to take place on his return from this voyage, as they were married by special licence in Clifton just one week after Thomas's ship docked from Quebec. The witnesses on their marriage certificate include Elizabeth's uncle and her sister's husband, who must also have been in Bristol at the time.

Elizabeth must have known whom she was marrying though, and that Thomas had to earn his living at sea, so after Christmas and New Year together, they were to be parted again . . .

1855

Thomas joined the twenty four strong crew of the 'Louisa', an eight-hundred ton vessel which left Bristol on 8th January for Quebec, arriving back in Sheerness on 16th July, a round trip over six months. Another turn around time of two weeks again for Thomas, who must have been pleased to see Elizabeth for the first time since their 'honeymoon' back in December. Mary Ann Slade was obviously conceived at this time, as she was born nine months later when Thomas and Elizabeth moved back to Appledore to set up home together.

In the meanwhile Thomas returned to the 'Louisa', which left again on 31st July, and

(Bristol Shipping Gazette and Market Circular)

EMIGRATION TO CANADA.
LOADING AT BRISTOL FOR QUEBEC,
THE Fine Fast Sailing Coppered Ship.
LOUISA, A 1.,
1,200 Tons Burthen,
CHARLES HOWES, Commander,
To Sail in July.
This Ship is noted for making quick voyages; she will be comfortably fitted up, and thoroughly good provisions supplied. As only a limited number of Passengers will be taken, early application for Berths should be made to
MARK WHITWILL and SON,
Ship Owners and Brokers,
Grove, Bristol.

returned to Bristol on 10th December, where the master recorded the crew as being:

(Public Record Office)

Elizabeth, being pregnant at this time, obviously had to give up work, and must have persuaded Thomas to return to North Devon, where they created a permanent home for themselves in Irsha Street, Appledore, in preparation for a new family member.

1856

Thomas and Elizabeth's first child (Mary Ann) was born in Appledore in April 1856, and was christened the following month.

We haven't proved that Thomas made any long sea voyages after returning to Appledore, however his service record does indicate he served on a ship called the 'Bacchus'. This could well be true, as the 'Bacchus' was a three-hundred ton barque trading from Bideford to Prince Edward Island at the time.

Certainly after a while Elizabeth insisted on her husband staying at home, even though this would mean a loss of a good source of income, and a reduction in their living standards.

IT IS SAID THAT Elizabeth, although living in poverty, was a born leader and was determined to make something of herself. She had the typically aggressive characteristics associated with the Kingdon family, which is probably where Mary Ann got her determination from. No-one dared contradict or answer Elizabeth back when she gave an order, but she was respected by all that knew her. It was said about Thomas (by his grandson) that he had a voice like a roaring lion, but underneath he was loveable and easy going, with a heart of gold; and of Elizabeth he said that she had a marvellous character, and plenty of go in her, in fact she ruled the family like a queen. She can be remembered sitting in her armchair giving her orders, and she used to sit in a black satin dress, with a white hat on and a gold chain around her neck, in fact she seemed to be the finest lady that was ever seen.

Eventually Thomas and Elizabeth purchased some fishing boats, and together with their other children (they had five boys and six girls) managed to make a living by fishing the

Taw and Torridge rivers. Elizabeth gradually built up a business of selling fish, and made her own markets with the help of contacts in London, in fact she became an agent selling fish for other local fishermen, and after a time had built up enough money to buy their own house. To illustrate her character, the following appears in the local paper in 1866....

CHARGE OF ASSAULT

"Elizabeth Slade, of Appledore, was summoned for assaulting George Williams, a boy eight years old. Defendant admitted striking the boy twice, but he pushed a cart down a hill, and nearly ran it over her little child. She spoke to him, and he then threw a stone and struck her in the head.

She then corrected him as a 'mother'; – Case dismissed."

Bideford & North Devon Gazette, 10th July 1866

Thomas also seems to have spent some time in Court. It would seem as though he was summoned for illegal fishing with six other men in 1862, as reported in the local paper. The rule of not netting salmon between Saturday noon and Monday morning was considered extremely important in order to allow the salmon upstream to spawn, thereby helping fish stocks to be conserved.

"After hearing the arguments for the case, the bench retired to consider their decision, and in the meantime the Court was entertained with the satires of the fishermen, directed against Captain White, Mrs Slade (a fish seller), also contributing. Thomas Slade wished Captain White was obliged to go down opening raw mussels, as he had been forced to, to get something to eat.

The Bench on their return, considered the case proved against two of the party: Richard Ross and Richard Hare, and they were fined £1, and their nets were forfeited."

Bideford & North Devon Gazette, 10th July 1862

Thomas Slade was therefore acquitted, as he was not proved to be actually involved in the fishing, but the atmosphere in the Court does

Fishing has been a part of the community of Appledore for centuries, and these fishermen in the 1920s are continuing a trade that goes back into pre-history. Here salmon are being caught using a net tethered to the shore at one end, and rowed around in a large semi-circle until the net is pulled in, and the fish loaded into the boat. (National Maritime Museum, Greenwich, London)

seem rather rough and ready compared to what would be expected today.

Whatever else Thomas and Elizabeth did in their lives is not generally recorded. They lived in Irsha Street, had eleven children and twenty-five known grand-children, and worked hard earning a living fishing from the river, until Elizabeth died in 1899 and Thomas eight years later. Their grave stands at the top of Appledore churchyard, in a prominent position overlooking the river.

Not surprisingly, some of Thomas's sons followed him into the seafaring trade, and it is the story of one of them: **William Kingdon Slade**, that will be told next.

WILLIAM KINGDON SLADE

AS SOON AS HE WAS old enough, William Kingdon Slade (born 1865) was sent to sea to make his living. However, as he had already had a hard existence on the sea since early childhood this did not come unnaturally, as he was already quite experienced in taking sailing boats out to sea over Bideford Bar, and had a good knowledge of the river Torridge and its estuary.

He first started to learn about being a seafarer on the brigantine *'Danube'* with George Quance as mate, but then became mate himself on a vessel called the *'Hawk'*. He progressed in 1891 to becoming Master of a seventy ton ketch called the *'Francis Beddoe'*, which was owned by Philip Harris who founded a successful ship-repair business in Appledore.

The *'Francis Beddoe'* (built in Pembroke-shire in 1877) was never owned by the Slade family, but does have an interesting place in the Slade family history, because of an event that happened in 1891.

WILLIAM KINGDON SLADE had been master of this vessel for less than a month, at the young age of 25, and the boat had been trading to Southern Ireland and Cornwall, but had yet to be brought back to Appledore since it had been bought by the Harris family. In March 1891 she was in Gloucester, and bound to take a cargo of salt to Bideford. Very soon after she had departed Gloucester, the whole of south west Britain was swept by a gale of exceptional ferocity, made much worse by being accompanied by heavy snow. Ships were wrecked all around the coast, and many seamen lost their lives. The account of this story was told to his son on board their ship the *'Alpha'* some years later, and is recounted here . . .

"The 'Francis Beddoe' was only eight years old when she was bought, and had been trading to St Agnes since her purchase and now for the first time she was bound to Bideford with a cargo of salt from Gloucester. She sailed on 7th March 1891. One or two others left the Bristol Channel area at the same time besides some Cornish vessels and in the ensuing blizzard in which a heavy easterly blew, quite a number of ships were lost with all hands. Some of the sailors died from exposure. Men were found after the gale wrapped up in sails, all dead. One of the well known Appledore sailors was ordinary seaman in a schooner that tried to find the land off Coombe Martin; she struck the rocks and sank. The crew got in the boat and followed the land wash till they reached Coombe Martin and were safe. These were the lucky ones. The 'Jane & Sarah', Captain Ayres, found smooth water which turned out to be Bude bay. She anchored and rode out the gale. One or two Appledore ketches got in over the bar just as it started. Again these were lucky to be home. The snow in Appledore piled up above the window sills of the houses and before the doors could be opened they had to be dug out.

After she left Sharpness on the 7th, the 'Francis Beddoe' ran down Channel. It had started to snow heavily on the morning of the 8th and it was like a blanket of snow all around. When William judged her far enough down he hauled in towards the south shore. Suddenly he realised he was in a race of tide and a heavy sea, so decided to heave to, in the hope that it would soon clear, but there was no clearance so hour after hour she drove with only a balance reef mainsail and storm jib, The night wore on and then another race of tide and enormously heavy sea. His mate was Philip Quance, an elder brother of George Quance, and an experienced sailor. They agreed it must be the south end on Lundy, but could do nothing but wait until it cleared and moderated enough to carry sail in order to get her under command. The mizzen was blown away and the damaged canvas furled. The night of the 8th passed. She still remained hove to on the starboard tack with the sea breaking on board all over her. The third hand gave up the struggle and laid down in the cabin refusing to do any more. The 9th March passed and the lights were lit but the sea was so bad they couldn't be used in their proper places because of the danger of losing them. The mate who wasn't a very robust man, now showed signs of exhaustion. During the night of the 9th the mate laid down in the cabin and was unable to do any more. There was no fire on board and water everywhere. Wet and miserable they slept not caring whether the little vessel floated or sank. Fortunately being nearly new, she was tight as a bottle so there was no pumping to be done. From the night of 9th onwards father was alone to face the elements. Altogether he was continuously on deck for four days and nights. He dare not sleep because he was afraid he wouldn't wake again. The situation was indeed desperate.

On the night of 11th the sky suddenly opened and for the first time since the gale started he could see a distance from the ship. Suddenly without warning, he saw a glaring starboard light and realised it would be dangerous. He managed to light the port side lamp which was red. He held it up so that it could be seen by the approaching ship. They came closer and closer until just as it seemed as if she was bound to run him down he saw her port light and she passed clear but only just

clear. The wash from her bow filled the lee side of the Francis Beddoe's deck, and father in his own words dropped on his knees and thanked God for deliverance from certain death. This proved to be a big full rigged ship running out of the Bristol Channel under her lower topsails. Soon after, the sky closed in again and the remainder of the night passed. On the morning of the 12th the sun broke through and the gale abated. There was nothing in sight. He managed to wear the ship to bring her round on the port tack, and lashed the helm amidships so that she would head reach slowly. He went to the cabin, rubbed some paraffin in the limbs of the crew and left them asleep. He also rubbed himself all over. He got into his bunk and went to sleep. After some hours he awoke and yelled out in agony; every limb was cramped and stiff. Eventually they all recovered enough to set the sails. The vessel fetched up into St Ives Bay and it was decided to work up the Cornish coast. The mizzen was loosened and with palms and

William Kingdon Slade
(1865-1942)

needles they set to work on it. It was soon in working order for fine weather only. In due course they reached Bideford bar.

In the meantime the family had given up all hope of his survival. Plans were being made for the children to be shared among the other members of the family so that mother could go out to work for a living. My grandfather had a telescope and he could often be found scanning the bay to follow the movements of ships. He could tell the name of a ship by the cut of the sails or the stand of the masts. He was doing this when he saw a strange ketch approaching the bar. The news soon travelled around and all rushed to the little yard called Ducks Alley. It was a point where the bar and a lot of the bay could be seen. Yes, they all saw this ship but the Francis Beddoe wasn't a ship they knew. Hope revived again but the suspense was intolerable and grandfather could stand it no longer. He went home and burst into tears. As this strange vessel approached they suddenly decided that those on board were not strangers by the way they came in. It must be local men, and therefore the Francis Beddoe could be this ship. The men of the family got a boat and boarded her. The crew were brought ashore and put to bed while the ship proceeded to her discharging berth at Bideford in charge of her new crew."

The Merchant Schooners: Basil Greenhill

A remarkable story, which may possibly have been embellished in the telling, but the local paper reported the blizzard as follows:

"*Scarcely within living memory has so heavy a fall of snow occurred as that which commenced about 3:30 on Monday afternoon and continued at intervals until Tuesday evening. To add to the severity of the weather, a strong gale blew* causing immense drifts and reducing the snow to a fine powder that found its way into every cranny and crevice. The past week has been one which will be memorable for very many years. On the sea this blizzard wrought fearful havoc, and wrecks attended with frightful loss of life, are reported on the coasts of South Devon and Cornwall. There were four wrecks in Start bay alone when fifty three lives were lost. In our own immediate neighbourhood, fortunately there have been no such disasters.*

North Devon Gazette, 17th March 1891

As far as William Kingdon Slade's story is concerned, this last sentence seems to be a rare case of journalistic under statement!

It is apparent from this story that William was a hardened man, especially when it came to looking after a boat at sea in all conditions. He was illiterate, never having gone to school as a child. However the wife he chose made up for his shortcomings in these respects. **Rosina Annie Harding**, herself the daughter of a sailor, who had spent much of her childhood sailing with her father Richard Harding on his vessels.

"She was taught the compass and how to steer by it, how to trim the sails by the wind or going off the wind, but better still she knew the land and sets of tides according to the time it ebbed or flowed. She also became a good judge of weather conditions; in fact she soon knew enough to be left in charge of the watch while her father slept.

As soon as she was able, she was sailing in the 'Francis Beddoe', charts, parallel rulers, dividers, etc, all fitted out and soon the way to use them came easily enough, but Rosina still kept her job as chief scribe. William sent her all the money he

Rosina Annie Abigail Slade (nee Harding) 1865-1964

could lay hands on and she saved all she could. It was the proudest day of her life when she went to the bank with a baby on her arm to deposit her savings and look at her first bank book.*

Women under Sail: Basil Greenhill & Ann Giffard

Eventually enough money had been put aside to buy their own house, and this they did in Westcroft Terrace, Irsha Street; and by 1895 they also saved enough to buy a half share in a ketch (the *'Heather Bell'*). The other half of this vessel was bought by William's mother Elizabeth, so it is likely that she was able to encourage him, and to give him full say in how the vessel was run.

Hard work it certainly was running a sailing ship, taking her to sea in all weathers, being responsible for the crew and their safety, navigating the vessel, and for finding a cargo and agreeing a price for transporting it. It was also necessary to help in loading and unloading it when in port, often with a deadline of a tide window to meet, otherwise another boat would beat you to the next port where you knew another cargo was waiting, and you would lose out to others who were quicker off the mark. Add to that the discomfort of life in the rudimentary accommodation provided in a small ketch, the poor food, the inadequate protection against the wind and the weather, and the backbreaking task of working the winches and heavy gear, and you have the recipe for a tough working life. William drove his crews hard though, and even his son said about him that: *'He was very very hard in every way. I had to toe the line, and nobody on board dared say anything to him, there were no back answers, when he gave an order, they had to jump to it. He was very dour, I never knew him laugh in all my life'.*

The ketch 'Heather Bell'. (National Maritime Museum, Greenwich. London)

In 1922, the *'Heather Bell'* was moored in the small pier harbour at Coverack near the Lizard in Cornwall, when she was caught by a very heavy south-easterly gale during a high spring tide, and she broke free from her moorings. William, who was sailing on the *'Haldon'* at the time, was moored not far away in Helford harbour with his son William James Slade, so they went to Coverack to assess the situation, and borrowed a hawser from the lifeboat station to make her fast again. They attached the hawser, and the crowd on the harbour managed to haul the boat back to the pier, as the ship ran forward and back with the sea. Eventually she was re-moored, and the tide receded, and so she became grounded for the night.

She was tied up as securely as possible, and it was felt that she would now be safe. However the gale was freshening, and during the next tide she broke adrift from the pier. The ropes had held, but the gale was so fierce, the granite mooring posts were pulled out, together with part of the pier.

She blew out of the harbour, and grounded on the rocks outside, becoming a total wreck. This was a dramatic end to a fine vessel, and if you visit Coverack today, you will still see where one of the granite mooring posts on the harbour wall was pulled out, and the hole made good, but the post never replaced.

OVER THE YEARS William Slade also bought and ran other sailing vessels:

- *'Alpha'*, bought in 1897, and kept for 16 years;
- *'Ulelia'*, bought in 1899, and kept for 17 years;
- *'Trio'*, bought in 1909 and kept for 10 years;

The ketch 'Heather Bell' wrecked outside the harbour at Coverack, Cornwall in 1922.
(National Maritime Museum, Greenwich, London)

- *'Elizabeth Jane'*, bought in 1910, and kept until she was lost in mysterious circumstances six years later . . . .

The *'Elizabeth Jane'* was an eighty-eight ton Schooner built in 1875 at Connah's Quay and bought jointly by George Quance and William Kingdon Slade. After George Quance's death, William Slade continued to trade with the *'Elizabeth Jane'* into the First World War, but with a hired Master and crew, when in 1916 she was lost with all hands in circumstances that are today still unknown.

1916, being in the middle of the war years, was noted for heavy shipping losses due to 'U Boat' activity all around the British and Irish coasts, and it is surmised that the ship was lost from an encounter with a German 'U Boat'. However this vessel is not referred to in any of

the war records for the period, which are fairly comprehensive, as the authorities kept strict lists at the time. It has been determined that the ship went down around 26th September 1916 off Queenstown, the port of Cork in Southern Ireland, however the only reference to this in any of the North Devon papers is a meagre paragraph under the local news section . . .

"News received at Appledore last week from Queenstown states that the ketch 'Elizabeth Jane' was a complete wreck in ten fathoms of water. Nothing is known of the crew, two of whom belong to Appledore, and the other to Braunton. The owner is Captain W Slade of Appledore."
North Devon Journal, 5th October 1916

Oddly, the names of the crew are not mentioned; and neither of the daily papers published in Cork at that time makes mention of the loss of this vessel, and of three sailors' lives being lost in the waters off this Southern Irish town, which is even more surprising.

This raises the following questions:

- What caused the vessel to sink?
- Why wasn't it reported in the local papers?
- Who saw it sink, if all the crew were drowned?

We know that the vessel wasn't wrecked on the coast, as the report indicates that it was lost in ten fathoms. However, two weeks later, the North Devon papers reported the death of the crew member from Braunton:

"Mr Skinner, of Mill Stile, Braunton, has received the sad news that his grandson Arthur J Skinner, aged 23, who was a member of the crew of the Appledore ketch 'Elizabeth Jane' (Capt. Handy) when she foundered off the Irish coast some few weeks ago, lost his life in the disaster, his body having been picked up on October 10th at Bally-Cotton, and was interred in the southern Graveyard on October 15th."
North Devon Gazette, 24th October 1916

The other members of the crew from Appledore who lost their lives in the disaster did not have their deaths reported in the local papers, probably because their bodies were never recovered, which seems to be borne out by there being no recorded burials for them locally. The names of this crew are however recorded on the 'Roll of Honour' memorial in Appledore church, which lists among the Mercantile Marine casualties:

- George Handy – 'Elizabeth Jane'
- Nathaniel Williams – 'Elizabeth Jane'

Their names can also be found on the Commemorative window in the church, and on the War Memorial outside the church gates. George Handy was a forty year old mariner who lived in Meeting Street, with a wife,

Appledore War memorial.

curiously also called Elizabeth Jane (nee Goodwin). Nathaniel Williams was aged fifty, but any further details of this accident are unknown because of the curious lack of mention of it in any sources.

IT CANNOT BE SAID that William Kingdon Slade ever really retired from the sea; he made fewer and fewer voyages as he got older, and spent more time running the business from home, and keeping an eye on his children, and more importantly his ships. In 1923 when he was beginning to spend less of his time at sea, he decided to do something worthwhile for his children, and made the decision to build a house for each of them in Appledore. A row of six terraced houses was therefore built in Myrtle Street, one for himself and one for each of his children, who must have been extremely grateful for this generous act. Indeed it was certainly not within most parent's

William Kingdon Slade and his family photographed here in 1905. He is standing at the back, with his wife Rosina seated. The children are, from the left: Elizabeth (4), William James (13), Mary (7), baby George (1), and at the back: Rosina (16) who died in 1908, and Hilda (18). On the right is Edwin (10), who died in the flu epidemic of 1918.

ability to be able to make such a gesture, and after a lifetime of scrimping and saving must have been a hard decision, but worthwhile to do something with the money which he had fought hard to earn over his working life.

Of his children (six girls and four boys, of whom only five survived to adulthood) **William James Slade** was the eldest son, and was therefore earmarked to take over from his father when he retired. He became not only a successful master in his field, but also, through his later writings, well known as a contemporary recorder of a way of life which was vanishing from the modern world.

William Kingdon Slade died in 1942, but his wife Rosina lived to be a grand old lady of ninety-nine, just failing by six weeks to reach the magic age of one-hundred. She was possibly the only woman from Appledore to take such an active part in the life of her husband, at a time when it was not the done thing to do a man's job, especially such a demanding one as seafaring. Part of the book '*Women under Sail*' was written about her life at sea, and is a story of a remarkable woman. She died in 1964, exactly as it states in the final words of this book: 'fully conscious, sensible and unafraid'.

WILLIAM JAMES SLADE

IT WOULD PERHAPS have been difficult for William James Slade (whom we will subsequently call Billie, as most people who knew him did) to have gone into any other trade. The options open to him were certainly slightly more than a century earlier, but still extremely limited in a seafaring town. He always said that he had a stormy entry into life, as he was born during a north west gale, when his father was away at sea, and he came home to find that he had a son.

Billie was first taken to sea when he was a few months old, in his mother's arms. She was also an experienced sailor, and for a month every year he voyaged with his parents, and learned the craft of seafaring from a very early age. His mother after a while had a larger family to look after and had to stay at home more, and so Billie was taken by his father as often as possible. Schooling was compulsory, and had to be attended during the rest of the year, even though Billie's father William did not see the need. After all he had managed throughout his life being fairly illiterate, and probably felt that his son could do the same. Indeed Billie recalls his father throwing his books overboard if he caught him reading them; so he had to hide his books, and continue to learn when his father wasn't around. After a while though, William seemed to have found Billie's knowledge useful, and thereafter compelled him to administer the ship's business, accounts and chartering as well as acting as an unpaid member of the crew.

Despite being hard, there were times when fun was had, but only when Billie's mother Rosina was around, as he recalled on one occasion:......

"We'd got mackerel lines over the stern, and I hated salt mackerel, but of course if father could catch them, we had to eat them. Well mother knew I didn't like them, but I had to put the lines out as soon as it was dawn. When mother came up on deck, she asked me if I didn't like mackerel, what did I want to catch them for? Well, if father was to come up on deck and find me without the lines going, there'd be deuce to pay; so she told me to go down and get a salt one, and hook it on, and throw it out on the end of the line. So I did, and when father came up, he noticed that there seemed to be a fish on the line, and told me off for not attending to the lines properly. He started pulling it in, and when he saw the mackerel come above water, he said 'This fish has been dead for hours' (actually it'd been dead for a week!), and he threw it on deck in a rage. Mother never turned a hair, and said 'Billie, you've caught a dead one' and laughed and laughed until she cried, but not father. I made a bee-line for the rigging, because I knew what was coming, and he nearly caught me, but I was up there before he could get to me. He followed me up though, and I had to go across the jump stay where he couldn't get me, and all the time mother nearly dying, and saying 'Tis a dead one you've caught Billie'. He saw what had happened fairly quickly though, and retreated looking foolish, but I always had to watch out for his quick temper."
BBC Radio interviews, 1962

Billie left school, after passing a leaving exam, which although he was the youngest in the group of sixty, he managed along with only eight others, and so at the age of twelve entered the full time world of work. He had done this however without his father being aware, and William only found out when he came home to find Billie with his bag packed ready to join his ship (the ketch 'Ulelia'). He became a permanent member of the small crew, and was subsequently paid the sum of one shilling per voyage as pocket money. As

This picture taken in 1905 below the old Quay at Appledore, shows three young Slade boys working on the tarring of one of the fishing boats of their grandfather Thomas Slade. They are Billie (left), and his cousins Thomas (centre) and Richard (right). All of these boys went on to become masters and owners of ketches trading from Appledore, and it is remarkable to see a picture of them all together from this date.
(National Maritime Museum, Greenwich, London)

the ship's boy, he had to wake up before anybody else in the morning, light the fires, and prepare the breakfast. After that, the mess in the cabin had to be cleared up, and then get up on deck to start the dinner going in the galley. Then there would be working the winch to load the cargo, and the fire had to be tended, and the washing up done, and if there was time when this was all done, then there were many other jobs which could be given to a boy to do.

The food on board was monotonous: for breakfast, one day they would have a couple of slices of bacon, the next it would be salt cod, and the next maybe Quaker oats, and then it would be back to bacon again. For dinner, if they were in harbour, maybe they would be lucky and have a bit of fresh beef, with potatoes or vegetables, but quite often at sea, bread and

jam or ship's biscuits would be the order of the day, and the usual salted fish.

Billie progressed well, but without a single word of praise from his father, who took it for granted that his son would follow him wherever he led, and would put up with whatever conditions were thrown at him. At the age of fourteen he was able to navigate the ship, and was for the first time left to plot a course and to take the boat into the harbour at Dingle in Ireland all by himself, no doubt with his father keeping a close eye, but of course without a murmur of praise for this achievement.

Billie continued on board his father's ships, and soon replaced the deck hand, and then the able seaman, and by the time he was seventeen, his father had just bought the '*Elizabeth Jane*', and Billie now became first mate on board her. But as Billie recalls, because they were always short-handed, only being able to afford to run the vessel with three men, he was still charged not only with the task of the cooking, but also with all the duties that the mate had to do as well. He was responsible for navigating, and had to be able to tell the exact position of the vessel on the chart after having been out of sight of land for several days. He learnt about tidal currents, and how they change at the different states of the tide, in fact everything that a coastal seaman needed to know in order to operate a vessel in inland waters.

At one time the Insurance Society was informed that William was sailing the 'Elizabeth Jane' with a boy of seventeen for mate, and the club objected to this. William arranged for a letter to be sent to them saying that he would agree to Billie being subjected to any examination they wished, and that he would guarantee he would pass it. As most of the committee were retired local sailors, who knew Billie Slade's record, they agreed that he was indeed capable of sailing a vessel without the need of any further tests, so the matter was accepted then and there.

Then in 1911, they had berthed the vessel in Ilfracombe harbour, and travelled home for a week-end, and Billie's father suddenly said: *'I'm retiring this trip'*, and Billie asked him who was going to take over. *'You are of course, you're going to take over'*. And so at the age of nineteen years and four months Billie Slade became Master of his own coasting vessel, William Kingdon Slade stayed home in Irsha Street, and Billie travelled back to Ilfracombe to take charge. His first voyage as Master must have been momentous for him, not only for having sole responsibility for the vessel, her cargoes and her crew, but also because of the sad news which reached him upon reaching Ballinacurra in Ireland. This was in September 1911, and the news was passed to him from another ship that his favourite uncle (George Quance) had died in a boating accident. Billie had always been a favourite of George and Mary Ann Quance, and they had encouraged him in his education, and it was most upsetting to hear of his death, especially when so far from home. The only comfort was the knowledge that George had lived just long enough to see him become Master of his own vessel.

APPLEDORE IN THOSE DAYS was a hive of industry. There were crowds of little sailing vessels from the Quay right up and down as far

(National Maritime Museum, Greenwich, London)

as you could see and a forest of masts when you looked out from the Quay. The vessels kept the shipyards going, and all the men that worked in the yards depended on the ships for their living, with repairs and new ships being built. The money earned was spent in the local shops in Appledore and Bideford. In fact it was said (by people in Appledore) that they kept Bideford going in those days, and that Bideford people were jealous of the fact that Appledore was thriving so much.

When Christmas came, all crews tried to arrange their cargoes so that they could be home in Appledore at the end of December. Some crews were obviously unable to make it, but Christmas was considered the one time of year when all of the family should be together, but if trade was good, it could not happen at any other time of year. The ships would congregate in the river until there wasn't a berth left, and they filled up the river as far as you could see. After the festivities were over, and the tide was right, all of the vessels would be likely to want to leave at the same time, and the immense flurry of activity must have seemed like rush hours are for us today, as up to a hundred boats would all try and leave together. They would be pushing each other apart with paddles and oars and boathooks to avoid collision. The forest of masts would be replaced by countless sails, all trying to catch the favourable wind, and be out at sea. If there was insufficient wind in the estuary, the vessels would have to be towed out, with the ship's boat towing from the front with two men rowing, and a length of rope fastened to the bowsprit end. Hard work for the rowers, but vessels of up to two-hundred tons could be manoeuvred out of the estuary in this manner; probably a good way of working off some Christmas excesses! The sight of so many vessels leaving on one tide must have been dramatic, and the silence they left behind in Appledore must have been just as dramatic after the frenzy of activity in the town over the holiday period. With such a sudden change in the town's population, all thoughts at this time must have been in getting the men folk back out to sea, and the women folk getting back to their daily grind of cleaning and laundering and dressmaking.

Back out at sea, the work was hard and monotonous, with little respite for recreation or even small comforts. Billie Slade said that

The schooner 'Millom Castle' leaving Appledore.

(*National Maritime Museum, Greenwich. London*)

for twenty years he rarely knew what it was like to have a dry bunk to sleep in whilst at sea. His life at sea continued, but under the firm eye of his father, who was still really running the show. Together they inspected and bought a second-hand top-sail schooner called the *'Millom Castle'* whilst they were both in Cork in Ireland, and sailed it back to Appledore. (The *'Millom Castle'* was built at Millom in Cumbria in 1870 for local merchants, and therefore called after the nearby ruined castle). On the way back to Appledore she was found to be leaking so badly that they had to put into South Wales, and beached the boat so that an intensive search could be made. A bad plank was found and eventually replaced, and for twenty-five years after that she proved to be one of the driest ships that the family ever owned.

She carried cargoes wherever they were needed, amongst which were:

- Stone *from Newport to Lymington*
- China Clay *from Falmouth to Glasgow*
- Oats *from Ireland to Gloucester*
- Coal *from Lydney to Ilfracombe*
- Bricks *from Bridgwater to Bideford*
- Gravel *from Appledore to Cardiff*
- Cement *from London to Minehead*
- Manure *from Plymouth to Newport*
- Flour *from Cork to Garston*
- Grain *from Portishead to Swansea*
- Maize *from Avonmouth to Padstow*
- Barley *from Arthurstown to Cardiff*
- Steel borings *from Hayle to Bristol*
- Barbed wire *from Gloucester to Briton Ferry.*

The coastal vessels of the 19th and early 20th centuries were the carriers of bulk materials, which after the 2nd World War were almost completely replaced by road transport, but in Appledore they were the work-horses of

trade, and the main source of income for many of its families.

During the First World War, Billie Slade married May Whitton, who he had known since he was fourteen, when her family moved into the house next door in Irsha Street. May

William James Slade and his wife May, on the occasion of their golden wedding anniversary in 1965.

was two years younger than Billie, but their friendship had appeared to have ended when her family moved to Redruth in Cornwall where May's father had been appointed Baptist minister at the local chapel. Some years later however, when Billie was master on the *'Elizabeth Jane'*, he was moored in Hayle harbour, and remembering his friend who had moved to Cornwall, borrowed a bicycle and cycled to see her. He was welcomed by the family, and they soon became friends again. They became engaged not long after that, and were married by May's father in the Baptist Chapel in Redruth. They settled in Redruth temporarily, and eventually had five children (all boys) and a marriage that lasted over fifty years. Family ties with his father were strong though, and so he was eventually persuaded to move back to North Devon with his new family, where in 1919 they bought a house in

Bideford. This was done apparently with a certain amount of bargaining, and was all concerning a major change that was taking place in their industry.

Up until 1910, all the coasting vessels that were operating around the coast of Britain were sailing vessels entirely subject to the vagaries of the wind and weather. In this year however, a Braunton-owned ketch (the *'Bessie Ellen'*) was fitted with an auxiliary oil engine, and proved that a vessel equipped in this way could be more economical and reliable. Seeing that others were having an advantage in the trade, Billie persuaded his father to fit an auxiliary engine into the *'Millom Castle'*, and this was done, but only if he agreed to move back to North Devon, both of which happened in 1919.

This meant that new skills had to be learnt to cope with the repair and maintenance on an engine, as well as retaining the skills to run a sailing ship. In fact conditions became worse because of this, as Billie described:

"Whilst in harbour there was always plenty to do in the engine room besides having to work the cargoes in and out. The accommodation aft was crude and the living conditions miserable, because half of the cabin was taken for engine room space and the smell of diesel oil everywhere. There was no sleep at sea because of the excessive vibration and noise. Often the top of the flimsy deck-house leaked like a colander. But those days were happy because conditions were hard everywhere, and we knew no different life."
'Out of Appledore': W J Slade

However, the First World War brought about benefits from increases in the freight charges, which made business a little more prosperous, and the availability of better food also improved conditions considerably.

After a couple of years running the *'Millom Castle'* in this way it was found that because of less wear and tear on the sails and rigging, changes could be made to these to

The schooner 'Millom Castle'.

(National Maritime Museum, Greenwich. London)

enable the vessel to be run more easily. The main mast, which had recently been damaged, had to be repaired anyway, and after some consideration about cost, the vessel was re-rigged in a very unusual manner. Normally on a schooner the main mast is in the centre of the vessel (on a three-masted vessel), or at the back (on a two-masted vessel). In this case however, William Kingdon Slade arranged to save money by using what was partly already there, and the masts were arranged with the tallest at the front, and the smallest at the back. This was greeted with great amusement from the Appledore sailors, and when one of them commented that the ship looked like a 'set of jugs', the name stuck, and she was thereafter always referred to by this derisive nick-name. The last laugh however was with William Slade and Billie, who found that she handled extremely well with this rig, and until she was sold in 1932 she was one of Appledore's most profitable vessels.

(The vessel 'Millom Castle' rigged with masts of decreasing size from front to back, that resulted in her being said to look like a 'set of jugs').

In February 1922 however, Billie was to have his worst ever fight with the sea. He was on the 'Millom Castle' coming back from Ireland with a cargo of ore used in lead making, and this is so heavy and concentrated that a wooden sailing ship could be strained in conditions like this, and leaks can easily occur. The weather turned bad, and they were stuck in Southern Ireland for some weeks waiting for a suitable break to enable them to sail. They eventually made it to sea, and took all precautions they could in securing all items and reefing the sails as much as possible, but the gale then became increasingly worse again. Then the barometer reading fell further, and they entered a calm area, which must have been the eye of the storm. They needed to get into the Bristol Channel area before the coming storm hit, so they started the engine, but within an hour, the gale hit, and they were still out in the open sea . . .

"We ran lovely for about half an hour, when a huge sea broke over the port quarter, the helm seemed useless, and she was full to the top of the rails. In the hollow of the sea the main boom came in, and when it went out it broke in two, the gaff went in three pieces. The battens and hatch wedges were adrift and one end of the main hatch tarpaulin was off. The fore-end of the main boom with heavy iron reef attached was over the side, towing. It was sheering off and coming and hitting the side of the ship like a battering ram. Other running gear was washed overboard, tangling in the propeller, which finished the engine. The mainsail, of course, disappeared altogether. Then the fight started.

My brother and the mate, secured the ship's boat and the boom, and then nailed the battens and tarpaulins to the hatch combings to keep the water out. Most of this time they were waist-deep in water. All that day we kept running, and the boat, lashed to the lee rails, never once showed herself clear of the water. My crew was marvellous, they were like two drowned rats, but never once did they despair.

I think my mate had had enough, he was worn out. He suggested St Ives bay and let the lifeboat take us off. I thought for a few minutes and then said 'No, I won't lose the vessel while she will stay afloat.'

The next day we passed Lundy with a good offing, and I kept away for the Bristol Channel.

come through it?' The salt had corroded in the eyes of the rigging forty feet above the deck. 'The wind registered one hundred and eight miles an hour at the Scilly Isles during the gale, and you were not expected to live through it with such a heavy cargo.'"

'Out of Appledore': W J Slade

We now had the wind behind us, and I set the squaresail, but it was only on her about fifteen minutes when the yard broke in the middle, so down it came again.

Then we tackled the propeller. After an hour of patient struggle working the flywheel of the engine in gear just a little, and winching in the ropes, I made up my mind to start the engine. To my great satisfaction, after a second or two, it cleared itself and we motored past Barry and finally anchored off Portishead safe. We had had practically nothing to eat or drink for three days and nights, but when the tea was made, we couldn't drink it, because our drinking water was salt.

The next day father appeared on the scene and when he saw the state of our ship was in, he said 'Good God! How in the world did she

Notwithstanding the above battle, Billie had had a worse life-threatening experience during the First World War, on another ship that his father had bought during this period. William Kingdon Slade was in Cork in 1916 when he saw a fine schooner called the '*W D Potts*', and agreed to buy her. She was a fairly large schooner of some eighty-eight tons built at Pwllheli in 1879. Billie Slade took charge of her, and found her to be a good reliable vessel, but he was only to have her for less than a year…

In February 1917 he was in Falmouth, and loaded a cargo of china clay for Glasgow. It was a long voyage, but the freight charges were good, because merchant ships were in short supply due to Wartime activities. There were risks though, mostly from German 'U Boats'. Billie was sailing up the West coast of England, and had reached the Scottish borders about ten miles off the coast of Wigtownshire. They were in the company of a big full-rigged Norwegian ship called the '*Ivrig*', when a German submarine surfaced about one hundred yards away, and immediately opened fire without warning. They rushed to get out their boat, and had just got in and clear of the ship when all the yards and mast head came tumbling down, part of which knocked a hole in their boat. Luckily the ship's boy (Isaac Jewell) saw the periscope before the submarine surfaced, and was able to start launching the boat in relative safety, although the Germans kept firing on their ship, but this extra notice undoubtedly saved their lives.

They managed to get away from their sinking ship, but the hole in the boat meant that they were in trouble straight away. They had a frantic night in which they had to row twelve miles to Portpatrick, arriving six hours later after having spent the whole night baling out the boat with a hard hat. The sentry who challenged them upon landing, looked after them very well, especially after discovering that Billie Slade was in the boat, as he had known his grandfather Thomas Slade very well (It's a small world in the sailing community!).

After the First World War, freight prices went up, and business was relatively prosperous during the 1920s. William Kingdon Slade had seen his son William become successful after him, and was reaping the benefits of investing in ships over the previous twenty-five or more years. Investments were still being made in ships though, and two more second-hand vessels were bought, one in 1922 called the 'Haldon', and the other in 1930 called the 'M. A. James'. Both of these vessels provided good earnings for the Slade family, and Billie served on first one and then the other, right up until the Second World War. However, after the successful years of the 1920s, the depression years of the 1930s hit hard. Freight prices dropped to their lowest ever, sometimes to below the cost of carrying the cargoes, but there was no option but to continue, if only in the hope of finding a cargo at your destination that would at least make a meagre profit. The situation continued for several years in this manner, times were harder than they had ever

WIGTOWN SHIRE

Stranraer

Portpatrick

'W.D.Potts' sunk here by German U Boat.

X

Belfast

NORTHERN

IRELAND

'W.D.Potts' bound for Glasgow with a cargo of China Clay.

A model of the schooner 'W D Potts', made by W J Slade, and now on exhibition in the Liverpool Maritime Museum.

LIST C. & D.

ISSUED BY THE BOARD OF TRADE.
In PURSUANCE OF 57 & 58 VICT., c. 60.

W B & L (8)—6763—1000-2-6

LIST OF CREW,

AND OTHER PARTICULARS OF A

FOREIGN GOING or HOME TRADE SHIP

To be delivered to the Superintendent of a Mercantile Marine Office when the particulars are not rendered in the form of an Agreement and Official Log, or either.

Name of Ship.	Official Number.	Port of Registry.	Port No. and date of Register.	Registered Tonnage. Gross. Net.	Nominal Horse Power of Engines.
W. D. Potts	77419	Carnarvon	2 / 1878	Unknown 112	88	—

REGISTERED MANAGING OWNER.

NAME.	Address (State No. of House, Street and Town).
W. K. Slade	13 Myrtle St Appledore Devon

Commencement of Voyage or Half-year.		Description of Voyage or Employment.	Termination of Voyage or Half-year.	
Date.	Place.		Date.	Place.
Jan 1st 1914	Falmouth	Coastwise	May 1st	At Sea Sunk by enemy Submarine

PARTICULARS OF ENGAGEMENT.
To be filled in when the Agreement is not delivered.

	Names of the Master and Crew.	Age.	Nationality. (If British, state birthplace.)	Ship in which Seaman last served, and year of discharge. Particulars to be entered only when not given upon Office Copy of Agreement. Year.	Name of Ship and Port she belonged to.	Date and place of signing Agreement. Date.	Place.	In what capacity engaged, No. of Certificate (if any), and No. of Reserve Commission or R.V. 3 (if any).
1	Master William James Slade	25	Appledore Devon		Same Ship		continuing	
2	John Evans	32	Appledore	1916	Same Ship	Jan 1st	Falmouth	Mate
3	Alfred George Evans	35	Teignmouth	1916	Same Ship	Jan 1st	Falmouth	A.B.
4	Isaac Jewell	16	Appledore Devon	1916	Same Ship	Jan 1st	Falmouth	O.S.
5	John Balsdon	35	Ilfracombe	1917	Adelaide of Fowey	Mar 13	Runcorn	Mate

	PARTICULARS OF DISCHARGE OR OTHER TERMINATION OF SERVICE. To be filled in when an Agreement is not delivered.				RELEASE. For use when Crew are discharged before a Superintendent and an Agreement is not delivered.		REPORT OF CHARACTER. To be entered when an Official Log is not delivered.	
Date of Joining.	Date, Place and Cause of leaving this Ship, or of Death. Date.† Place.† Cause.†			Balance of Wages due on Discharge.	Signatures or Initials of Official before whom the Balance of Wages was paid and Release and date.		Ability.	Conduct.
9	10	11	12	13	14	15	16	17
	1/5/17	at Sea	Ship Sunk by Enemy Submarine		William James Slade			1
Jan 1st	Mar 13	Runcorn	Discharged	20 0 0	John Evans	J.B.	V.G. V.G.	2
Jan 1st	1/5/17	at Sea	Ship Sunk by enemy Submarine	6 2 0	Alfred George Evans	J.B.	V.G. V.G.	3
Jan 1st	1/5/17	At Sea	Ship Sunk by enemy Submarine	4 2 8	Isaac Jewell	J.B.	V.G. V.G.	4
Mar 13	1/5/17	At Sea	Ship Sunk by enemy Submarine	9 10 8	John Balsdon	J.J.	V.G. V.G.	5

Crew list document for the 'W D Potts' on her fateful voyage in 1917. (Public Record Office)

been, and only improved when it got close to the Second World War, and suitable cargo carriers were harder to find.

A full account of the life of William James Slade can be found in his autobiography that he wrote in the late 1950s after his retirement, called 'Out of Appledore'. This contains extremely detailed descriptions of the life of a coasting seaman in the first half of the 20th century, from his first memories of being at sea, right up to the Second World War and beyond. The descriptions from the depression years in the 1930s are particularly vivid. Many vessels were laid up, and shipyards went into receivership from lack of business.

During the December of 1935, Billie and his crew were trying to keep the 'Millom Castle' working as hard as possible, in order to try and earn a meagre living. They found that Christmas was almost upon them, but they were in Southern Ireland near Kinsale, and had to put in to a remote quay at Oyster Haven for the holiday period. Billie said that it felt like being dropped into a huge dark pit - the hills surrounding them were heavily wooded, and about five times higher than the ship's masts, it was dark, and there were heavy gales blowing. On Christmas Eve, Billie had to walk five miles across the fields in the rain to Kinsale for provisions. He and his crew then spent Christmas Day and Boxing Day in this dark and gloomy location, waiting for the labourers to return after their Christmas break to start loading cargo into his ship. He says that was the loneliest Christmas he can remember.

In former times, when ships like these used sail power alone, a crew of five would generally be needed to run them, but with motors as well, it meant that generally a crew of three could just about manage. Any more would have made the trips uneconomic, although even with a small crew of three, these voyages could hardly be described as moneymaking.

The 'Haldon', although she could never be

described as a good-looking ship, seemed to have had a special place in the hearts of the Slade family. She soldiered on through good times and bad, was robust, and carried large cargoes for her size, and was therefore more profitable than most other vessels operating at this time. No doubt the profitability was also added to by the hard work that Billie Slade and his father put into her.

THE 'HALDON' was named after a place called Haldon, near Exeter, where there is a large wooded area of hills. In 1891 (remember the great storm and the battle that W K Slade had with the sea on the 'Francis Beddoe') great damage was done all around the south-west coast, and in the Haldon woods many trees were blown down. Some of the timber from these trees was taken to Hawke Brothers (shipbuilders) of Plymouth, and after seasoning, the timber was used to make two ships, one of which was called the 'Haldon' after the place where the timber came from. She was launched in March 1893, and after serving in Topsham, Southend, the Orkney Islands, and Haverfordwest, was bought by the Slade family in 1922 for £1200. Some changes to her were made in 1924, when she was converted from a two-masted ketch into a three-masted schooner, and again in 1930 when a more powerful engine was fitted.

She was almost lost in 1938, when she was involved in a collision off the coast of South Wales on the way back from discharging a cargo at Port Talbot, as Billie Slade describes:

"I had been off the deck about half an hour, when I heard the mate shout, 'Oh! My God! Realising something was wrong I jumped for the deck, reached the wheel as we struck a light oil tanker stem on into her port side. The crew were taking to the boat without bothering where I was. I yelled to them to stop lowering the boat, while I steered our ship clear of the other.

When I went forward to ascertain the

Form No. 10.

BILL OF SALE. (Individuals or Joint Owners.)

No. 79 (Sale).

Official Number	Name of Ship	No., Date, and Port of Registry
85955	Haldon	3/1920 Barnstaple

Whether a Sailing or Steam Ship		Horse Power of Engines, if any
Auxiliary Sailing		50

		Feet	Tenths
Length from forward part of stem, under the bowsprit, to the aft side of the head of the stern post	...	38	6
Main breadth to outside of plank	...	21	9
Depth from top of deck at side amidships to bottom of keel	...	9	

NUMBER OF TONS.

Gross	...	113 · 22		
Registered	...		76 · 88	

and as described in more detail in the Certificate of the Surveyor and the Register Book.

• I, *William Kingdon Slade, of Appledore in the County of Devon Master Mariner* _____

in consideration of the Sum of *Four hundred pounds* _____ paid to † *me* by *William James Slade*

of *Bideford in the County of Devon Master Mariner* _____

the Receipt whereof is hereby acknowledged, transfer *twenty four sixty fourths* Shares in the Ship above particularly described, and in her boats, guns, ammunition, small arms, and appurtenances, to the

said *William James Slade* _____

Further to ‡ *the said William Kingdon Slade* _____ for § *myself* _____ heirs covenant with the said

William James Slade _____ and ‖ *his* _____ assign, that ¶ *I* have power to transfer in manner aforesaid the premises hereinbefore expressed to be transferred,

and that the same are free from incumbrances**

In witness whereof I‡‡ hereunto subscribed *my* name and affixed *my* seal this *twenty fifth* day of *July* _____ One thousand nine hundred and *Twenty Two*

Executed by the above-named *William Kingdon Slade.*

in the presence of ††

Hilda Jane Lamey
Fairholme Street
Myrtle Street
Appledore
Devon
(Housewife)

William K. Slade

Bill of Sale Document for the purchase of the 'Haldon' in July 1922.

extent of the damage, I got a shock. She was
completely shattered down to the light water
mark. If she had been loaded, there is no doubt
she would have sunk like a stone. I entered the
forecastle and found water rushing in but no
more than we could cope with. The mate
suggested we let her sink and take to the boat,
but I couldn't do that without a struggle to save
her, so made up my mind to risk getting her
home. **"**

'Out of Appledore': W J Slade

Billie managed to get her back to Appledore, and then had to do even greater battle
with the insurance company in his claim for
payment. Eventually the *'Haldon'* was repaired,
although the repairs cost more than the money

paid by the insurance company, she was now a
much stronger ship, but became so just in time
for an even greater threat: the Second World
War.

During this period, merchant shipping
was almost as important as Naval shipping, as
it was vital to keep supplies flowing between
countries, but many of Billie's contemporaries
joined the Royal Navy to serve their country.
Billie kept trading in the *'Haldon'* although this
was not without many risks. Danger from
submarines and minefields were a continuous
threat, but for those who wished to keep
trading, freight prices virtually doubled overnight, so it became a worthwhile business again.
In 1940, an encounter with a stray mine, which
came within two feet of the *'Haldon'* almost

The *'Haldon' shown here in 1938 with a missing bowsprit and damaged bow, following a collision with an oil tanker in the Bristol Channel. William Kingdon Slade is on the far left of the picture surveying the damage.*
(National Maritime Museum, Greenwich, London)

An oil painting of the 'Haldon' *by William James Slade, painted in his retirement.* (Private Collection)

caused the end of this vessel again, and she was lucky not to have been blown out of the water.

She was however considered to be a lifeline for the Slade family in the event of a German invasion, when it was proposed that if England was invaded, the family could throw everything they had in her, and sail for America. Fortunately this did not happen, but the end of everything nearly came just as quickly as an invasion.

IN 1940, THE GOVERNMENT needed some of the old wooden sailing ships for defence purposes, mostly to be used as mooring stations for networks of barrage balloons to protect Britain's main ports. As most of these mooring points had to be in the water, the wooden vessels were just right for this purpose, and so a process of requisition orders were sent out to their owners. The '*M.A. James*' had already been taken away, with the promise that she would be returned in the same condition after the War. This left Billie

Slade with just the '*Haldon*', and all seemed lost, except for a slight error on the part of the Ministry of Defence, who sent the requisition order to Billie's father William Kingdon Slade in Myrtle Street. Billie's father informed him of this by telegram whilst he was in County Cork chartering a cargo for Lydney, but was determined to keep trading if at all possible.

He noticed that the requisition order had been sent to his father, who no longer owned any part of the '*Haldon*', and was therefore determined not to comply with an order he did not feel was necessary, so ignored the request and proceeded to Lydney with his cargo. He left the ship there being loaded, and returned to Appledore for the week-end.

"There I found all the requisitioned ships about to be surveyed, and most of them hoping for release. I had to have some conversation with the officer attached to the Admiralty for the taking over of these craft, really about the

'M.A.James', but during this talk, he asked where the 'Haldon' was lying, and I replied she is at Lydney, and I am her master. He said 'You were ordered to Appledore for survey'. I replied 'Did you send me a requisition telegram?' He looked up his list, and sure enough it was there, addressed to W Slade, Myrtle Street, Appledore, Devon. 'Well' I said, 'I'm afraid you've blundered in my case. I'm the owner of the 'Haldon' and she has nothing to do with the man you sent to. I'm W Slade, but my home is in Bideford'. After some argument, I and my ship were rejected. **"**
'Out of Appledore': W J Slade

So Billie Slade was given back the freedom to trade with the '*Haldon*', and continued to do so, until September 1943, when it became

obvious that his eyesight was not as good as it should have been, mostly due to an injury he received during an air raid on Avonmouth earlier in the War. He handed over control of his ship to his mate, William Cox, and the next year sold her for £2500, more than twice as much as he paid for her.

He had made a good living with the '*Haldon*' for twenty-one years, and had accumulated enough capital to enable him to retire from the sea for good, at the age of fifty-two. He had had a hard life at sea, but that was not unusual in the trade in which he found himself, and this was compounded by him continually suffering from sea-sickness, which he described as a 'miserable affliction', but that he never let it get him down! He was at sea permanently for nearly forty years, no holidays were taken except for the usual Christmas breaks, and no time off for illness, apart from two months in Exeter hospital after he lost an eye in the early 1930s (he was chopping some wood with his brother when a shard came off the axe, and went into his eye - a glass one had to suffice thereafter).

This didn't stop him working in his retirement, making ship models, and doing paintings of the ships that he had sailed in and admired. In 1954 he was persuaded by Basil Greenhill (then director of the National Maritime Museum) to write his auto-biography, because Billie was the last of a line of coastal sailors, whose trade had almost completely disappeared, and he was therefore in the unique position to record this disappearing lifestyle for posterity. This he did for the next three years, and the text was subsequently edited down into the best-selling local book '*Out of Appledore*', first published in 1959, and again in three subsequent editions. Later he recorded a series of three half-hour programmes for BBC radio about his life at sea, and these were broadcast in 1962.

William James Slade proudly displaying one of the ship models constructed during his retirement.

Basil Greenhill writes of him:

"The Slade family had become the last owners of merchant auxiliary sailing ships in Britain. W J Slade's particular privilege has been to be almost the sole means of preservation of the way of life that men like him followed. His autobiography is a fascinating and most valuable record of social and maritime history in village England, and links us with a world we have completely lost."

Billie Slade never learnt to swim (like many of his contemporaries), and presumably feared the sea, but always knew he would have a natural end to life. He was right about this, as in many other things, and died peacefully in Bideford in 1982.

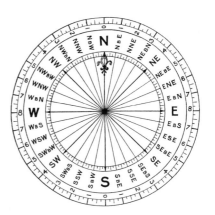

CONCLUSION

IT HAS ONLY BEEN POSSIBLE to tell about the lives of a few of the Slade family members in this book, but no doubt many others also had interesting stories to tell. A family tree has been produced on page 188 showing all the known descendants of William Slader since he moved to Appledore in 1777, and you can see they have become prolific, and have since spread far and wide.

The Slade family has made a significant contribution to the history of Appledore, and I hope that this book goes at least part of the way to show recognition of this.

SLADE Family Tree

Appledore, Devon

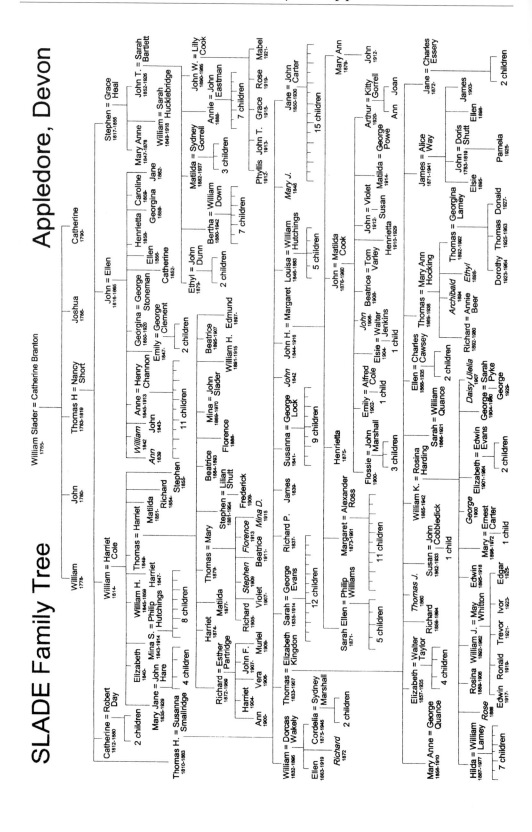

A car-free Quay complete with newly planted trees in about 1950. Nicholas Pevsner in his Buildings of England, wrote about Appledore: *"The compact streets of simple white-walled 18th and 19th century houses are a delight to explore, enhanced by their hillside setting rising gently from the estuary. The Quay, made in 1845, in place of private jetties, but widened and straightened (a pity) in 1939. Since then some inappropriate municipal planting has been undertaken. An informal array of houses of varying heights faces the water, several once provided with large upper floor windows to light sail lofts".*
(North Devon Museum Trust)

The Quay in about 1955, and the *'Kathleen and May'* is the only ship visible in the picture, indeed by this time she is one of the few surviving ships still operating from Appledore. The number of cars appearing on the Quay is also increasing, but it still looks a fairly tranquil scene.

In the 1930s, the Appledore Sailing Club was formed by local fishermen. The boats had clinker hulls eighteen feet long, and the single lug sails had to have no more than twenty-two square yards of fabric. Races were held on regatta days, and also on suitable summer evenings and Saturdays.
(North Devon Museum Trust)

A tranquil pastoral scene from the 1920s with two women (and presumably a photographer) enjoying a stroll just up the riverbank from Appledore. *(North Devon Museum Trust)*

The 'Kathleen and May' was the last trading schooner to operate from Appledore, and is therefore fondly remembered. This picture shows Captain Thomas Jewell on board her in 1955. He operated the 'Kathleen and May' until she left Appledore for the last time in 1960. She has since returned however, and is in the process of being restored in Bideford. After retirement, the BBC called upon Capt. Jewell to assist them in the making of the TV series 'Onedin Line', as no-one else with sufficient knowledge of sailing ships could be found to advise on sailing the ship used in the series. *(North Devon Museum Trust)*

A familiar landmark from Appledore for many years, the Yelland power station across the river near Fremington was built in 1952 to provide coal driven power to the National grid. The long jetty that ships used when delivering coal is still there, but the building itself was demolished in 1985.
(North Devon Museum Trust Collections)

This Viking longship was built by Alan Hinks yard in 1974, and is seen here 'under full steam' going past Appledore Quay, thankfully in a more friendly situation than when Viking longships were last seen in the area! *(North Devon Museum Trust)*

In 1968 the small shipbuilding yard of Alan Hinks completed the building of a replica of a 300 year old sailing ship called the *'Nonsuch'* for a Canadian company. She generated much interest from around the world in Appledore, and was the first of several similar commissions. She is seen here in full sail carrying out sea trials.

The boating pool below the Promenade was filled by the tide, and left a safe pool for children to sail their boats. The top of the iron ladder that went down to the beach can just be seen on the left of the picture, and the parents in this picture seem happy to watch their children playing safely here.
It was quite common to find exotic corals and other rocks on the beach here, as these were brought back by ships as ballast and dumped overboard at the end of their voyage. What remained of the boating pool was covered up by the construction of the car park in 1990. *(North Devon Museum Trust)*

To build replica ships in the 1960s and 1970s required forgotten trades to be re-learnt, although much of the expertise still existed in retired people in Appledore. The men here are Jo and Oswald Bennett, the last ship-riggers in Appledore, seen here working on the *'Nonsuch'* for Alan Hinks in 1968. *(North Devon Museum Trust)*

The new covered yard of Appledore Shipbuilders at Bidna being constructed here in 1970. It was a risky financial venture to build what was then the largest covered shipyard in Europe, and to make it viable its first commission had to be built at the same time as the yard. Here the dredger *'Pen Stour'* is being built in the partly finished shipyard. She was launched on 17th April 1970. *(North Devon Museum Trust)*

The replica model of the *'Golden Hind'* built at Alan Hinks yard in 1972, shown here in full sail. *(Beken of Cowes)*

No-one really knows how they blessed their ships before launching them in Elizabethan times, but this ceremony was carried out on the *'Golden Hind'* in 1972, albeit enacted for the local television cameras. The slip-ware jug being used in the picture is now in the Appledore Maritime Museum, and was made to commemorate another vessel's voyage in Victorian times, and may indeed therefore have been used for a similar purpose previously. *(D R Carter)*

Appledore Quay at the turn of another century, and heading into the future with a new raised promenade along the Quay-front. Apart from giving the village the protection and peace of mind that tidal flooding should be a thing of the past, it is also possible now to step back further and admire the buildings along the front from this extended vantage point. *(D R Carter)*

This colourful new wall sign was designed by local school children, and made by local craftsmen, as part of the 1999 Appledore Arts Festival. It perhaps represents the future of Appledore, not as a heritage village looking to the past, but as a centre for artistic creativity that will provide new interest in the town, by looking in a completely new and interesting direction. *(D R Carter)*

BIBLIOGRAPHY

Anglo-Saxon Chronicles – Anne Savage translation 1982
Anglo-Saxon England – F M Stenton 1971
Appledore Handmaid of the Sea – John Beara 1976
Bideford & North Devon Gazette
Bideford, Westward Ho! & Appledore Railway – Stanley Jenkins 1993
Boyhood Memories of Appledore – E R Carter 1989
British Directories – Gareth Shaw and Alison Tipper
Buildings of England – Nikolaus Pevsner 1952 and 1989
Cruel Coast of North Devon – Michael Nix 1982
Devon, A Century in Photographs – Devon W.I. 1997
Devon, 100 Years Ago – Frank Graham 1969
Devon and Cornwall Notes and Queries
Devon and Exeter in the Civil War – Eugene A Andriette 1971
Devon Harbours – Vernon Boyle 1952
Devon's age of Elegance – Peter Hunt
Devonshire – by Richard Polwhele 1977 edition
Devonshire Association – 1876 to 1996
Dictionary of Folklore, Mythology and Legend
Handbook of coins of the British Isles – Bradley 1982
History of Devon – Robin Staines 1986
History of Devonshire – Worth 1895
Industries of North Devon - Strong – 1889 & 1971 editions
Kelly's Directories
Last Bible Christians – Roger Thorne
Life of King Alfred – Asser 1959 edition
Lundy, Official Guide – F W Gade 1970
Lure of Contraband – J Weare Giffard 1920
North Devon - A Brief Maritime History
North Devon Coast – Charles G Harper 1908
North Devon Heritage Magazines – N Devon Heritage Trust
North Devon Story – Eric R. Delderfield 1952
Old Bideford and District – Muriel Goaman 1968
Out of Appledore – W J Slade 1959
Payne's Devon – Peter Hunt 1986
Prehistoric England and Wales, Penguin Guide – James Dyer 1981
Printed Maps of Devon - 1575 to 1837 – Batten and Bennett 1996
Shipwrecks of the Bristol Channel – Graham Smith 1991
Short history of England – Cyril Ransom 1901
Smugglers Britain – Richard Platt 1991
St Mary's Church, Appledore – Lester Yeo 1988
Survey of the County of Devon – Tristram Risdon 1811

The Merchant Schooners – Basil Greenhill 1951
Tidal Range – Nigel Melville 1990
Travels in Georgian Devon – Journals of John Swete 1997
Tudor and Stuart Devon – University of Exeter Press 1992
Two Rivers Meeting – Lois Lamplugh 1998
Two hundred year history of Appledore Shipyards – Len Harris 1992
Two Saxon Chronicles, parallel – Charles Plummer 1899
Victoria County History
Victorian & Edwardian Devon from old Photographs – Brian Chugg 1975
Westcountry Coasting Ketches – W J Slade and Basil Greenhill 1974
Westcountrymen in Prince Edwards Isle – Basil Greenhill 1967
Westward Ho!, Northam & Appledore Official Guide – 1955
Westward Ho! – Charles Kingsley 1855
Women under Sail – Basil Greenhill & Anne Giffard

People & Sources

Ashmolean Museum – Oxford

Barry Reference Library

BBC – Radio interviews with Capt. William James Slade 1962

Bideford and District Community Archive – Northam

British Library – London

British Newspaper Library – Colingdale

Cardiff Maritime Museum

Devon and Cornwall Notes and Queries

Devon County Record Office – Exeter

Family History Record Centre – London

Francis Frith Collection, Salisbury, Wiltshire, SP3 5QP.

Guildhall Library – London

Knights Photographers – Barnstaple

Liverpool Maritime Museum

National Maritime Museum – Greenwich

National Monuments Record Centre – Swindon

North Devon County Record Office – Barnstaple

North Devon Maritime Museum and Museum Trust

Public Record Office (crew lists, mariners records, maps collection, etc)

Royal Institution of Cornwall

Royal Naval Museum – Portsmouth

Swindon Reference Library

The Internet

Acknowledgements

My father Reg Carter (for having the insight to be born in Appledore)

Bill Wright (for his excellent illustrations)

Adrian Singer (for making the book look as professional as it does)

Dr Basil Greenhill (without whom, this book would not have been started, and whose answers to my untiring questions, have been greatly appreciated)

Pat Wiggett, Dr Alison Grant, and Barry Hughes (from the Appledore Maritime Museum, for their help and assistance)

Julia Dickmann (for encouragement, enthusiasm, and for checking my grammar)

Zena Woodley (for her knowledge on Copyright and the Welsh language)

Stephen Gadd (for producing a web-site for me)

My wife Jenny (for knowing when to keep out of my way, when to come and offer assistance, and for getting it right most of the time!)

All efforts have been made to contact the owners of the pictures included in this book, but if any errors have been made, then I humbly apologise.

ABOUT THE AUTHOR

I was born and brought up in Swindon, as a result of my father moving there from Appledore when he needed to find professional work. However, as a child visiting my grandparents each year at Easter, Summer and Christmas, I soon grew to know Appledore as my second home, and enjoyed not only being by the sea, but also exploring the narrow streets, as the picture below shows. Today we still have the house that was built by my great grand-father, and we look after it as part of our family heritage.

I am employed as an Architectural Project Manager for a large Retail Company, have a wife and two daughters, and in my spare time enjoy historical research, music, theatre, food (both cooking and eating), and helping my wife run her family history business.

Whether publishing this book will take my career in a new direction, only time will tell, but I would be pleased to hear any comments you have about it.

David Carter

NOTE FOR SECOND EDITION
I am indebted to all the people who have written to me after the publication of the first edition, with comments and congratulations; and to provide me with further snippets of information, many of which have been included in this edition. Please keep them coming!